Library of
Davidson College

THE GREAT GAMBLE:
THE BOEING 747

THE GREAT GAMBLE:
THE BOEING 747

The BOEING - PAN AM Project
to Develop, Produce, and Introduce
the 747

by
Laurence S. Kuter

THE UNIVERSITY OF ALABAMA PRESS

UNIVERSITY, ALABAMA

Copyright © 1973 by
The University of Alabama Press
ISBN: 0-8173-8700-5
Library of Congress Catalog Card Number: 73-37
All Rights Reserved
Manufactured in the United States of America

Contents

INTRODUCTION: THE BOLD VENTURE   vii

1 OBJECTIVES AND REALITIES   1
December 1965–June 1967

2 THE STRUGGLE FOR PERFORMANCE GUARANTEES   30
June 1967–September 1968

3 THE STRUGGLE FOR DELIVERY ON SCHEDULE   74
September 1968–December 1969

4 747 OPERATIONS AND GROWTH   101
January 1970–January 1972

Introduction:

The Bold Venture

This is the story of a businessman's risk that involved billions of dollars. It is the case history of the strenuous and sometimes tempestuous Boeing - Pan Am venture in producing and introducing the 747. It is a detailed account of the decision making and decision changing in two major corporations during five vigorous years.

In 1965, three days before Christmas, the president of the Boeing Company, Mr. William M. Allen, and the chairman and chief executive officer of Pan American World Airways, Inc., Mr. Juan T. Trippe, signed a statement of their respective intentions to build and to buy and operate the 747. Each of these executives entered into a project which, on failure, would unquestionably bankrupt his company or, on success, should assure the retention of leadership by his company in advanced high quality air transportation at relatively low cost.

To initiate the 747 project, the Boeing Company would have to commit over two billion dollars with no likelihood of retrieving much of it if the 747 should not prove to be an unquestioned success. Boeing would have to construct one of the world's largest buildings as a factory in which to build

INTRODUCTION

the 747. The location for the factory was an alder forest alongside Paine Field, an available World War II military airdrome, near Everett, Washington. To get large 747 parts to this factory, Boeing would have to build a rail spur from the main line in Seattle to the factory and special cars to carry the large parts from subcontractors' plants, and would have to arrange for the assignment of special locomotives to move those cars up the short steep grades to the factory. Investments of such magnitude were not likely to be recouped unless the 747 was a great success.

On Pan Am's part, that airline would have to commit to payments of well over five hundred million dollars and deliver fifty percent of all payments due Boeing for twenty-five airplanes six months before the delivery of the first 747. This huge advance payment was to be made before the Federal Aviation Administration could have tested the 747 to establish and certify its airworthiness or its suitability for airline operation. Five hundred million dollars was about twenty-five million dollars more than Pan Am's total passenger revenue for 1965, and that was the highest Pan Am had ever recorded. If it should develop that the first airplanes delivered after these huge prepayments turned out to be business failures, Pan Am's chances of survival would be very slim indeed.

Within these vast gambles there were lesser gambles which alone could make more timid souls tremble. For example, the decision was made rather early in the game that the cockpit of the 747 would contain no provision of any nature to carry a navigator or any facilities for sidereal navigation. Such facilities were essential in Pan Am's 707s and DC-8s and the FAA would not permit those aircraft to fly over oceans without a navigator in the crew. Pan Am and Boeing gambled that the AC Electronics Division of General Motors would produce, on time, an inertial navigation system which would be so

The Bold Venture

accurate and so reliable that a human navigator would be completely replaced by this technological innovation. At that time neither AC nor any other aerospace pioneer had ever built an inertial navigation system that the FAA would certify in lieu of a human navigator, nor had the Airline Pilots Association or any other union stated that they would operate such an airplane on long over-water flights without a skilled navigator.

There can be no question that each of these chief executives risked bankrupting his company by this venture and that each took the risk knowingly. On the other hand, if the 747 should prove to be as relatively successful as Boeing's 707 had been ten years before it, both companies could look forward to retaining world leadership and to years of corporate profits. There could be no doubt that this venture represented the biggest risk ever taken in the entire transport industry, perhaps in any business or any industry at any time. Herein is the story of that bold venture.

At the end of the first year of Pan Am's operation of the Boeing 747, it was evident that this huge project was not a failure. Analysis of the records of the first two years of operation of the 747 broadens the base of optimism in forecasting the eventual success of the project. However, its degree of success in competition with big new tri-jets and supersonic transports, while meeting the unforecast lag in global economy, will not be determined till later in the decade.

LAURENCE S. KUTER
General, USAF (ret. 1962)
June 1973   Executive Vice-President, Pan Am (ret. 1970)

CHAPTER I

Objectives and Realities

December 1965–June 1967

The optimistic and visionary objectives of the policy makers come face to face with the practical limits of aeronautical engineering.

The Genesis. The basic factors which led to the 747 project were the outstanding business successes of the two bold participants and their confident personal forecasts for the future of their companies.

Over some thirty years, Mr. Allen's company had achieved a series of brilliant successes in producing big propeller-driven and big jet aircraft including for the U.S. Air Force the B-17, B-29, B-50, the C-97 (the StratoCruiser), the B-47, B-52, KC-135, and for civil commercial aviation the spectacularly successful 707 series of pure jet and fan-jet transports. In the case of Boeing's civil jet transports, Pan Am had participated in their design and development and had bought and paid for the first substantial order. Most of the world's airlines followed closely behind Pan Am's lead.

For almost forty years Mr. Trippe's company had achieved brilliant success as the American leader in air transportation. Pan Am was first across the Atlantic, first across the Pacific, and first around the world. Its long series of other "firsts" in air transport are many indeed. Perhaps Pan Am's most remunerative "first" was the practice of collaborating with Boeing and being "first," for example, in offering the airline passengers of the world the great advantage of flight in the big pure jet transport—Boeing's 707—in 1958.

It was natural that these leaders who had known each other as Bill (Allen) and Juan (Trippe) for a couple of decades to team up on a project to build a new and advanced jet transport. They knew that the project was far too big for either company to handle alone. They knew that it was time to break through with new technologies to create a new concept of air transport for the '70s.

It was also natural that decision makers with such backgrounds and histories did not call for academic cost-effectiveness studies by their staffs or for series of alternatives to the objective to break through into the '70s with the new technology that would use the advanced high temperature, high by-pass fan-jet engines then under study in order to produce a still faster, still bigger and much better fan-jet air transport. In effect, each of these leaders had kept a running cost-effectiveness study currently in his mind. Each was sure that there was no alternative to the best and the biggest jet that the state-of-the-art could produce.

Economic Requirement. In early 1965, Pan Am still had twenty-seven propeller aircraft and one hundred jet transports, of which all were Boeing's except eighteen Douglas DC-8s. For several years Pan Am's forward planning had been based on an assumed annual increase in passenger traffic of twelve, fifteen, and twenty percent. Each succeeding year, these assumptions had proved to be too conservative. To meet the forecast increasing requirements for capacity, procurement programs were necessarily laid out for three or four years into the future. In early 1965 Pan Am forecast clear requirements for about six more long range and three short range (727) jets for 1966, some twenty-two long range 707s in 1967 and six more 727s and about seven long range 707s for 1968 to

December 1965–June 1967

bring the total of pure jet and fan jet aircraft to some one hundred and forty three. Beyond 1968, the tenth year that Pan Am would be operating the 707 type Boeing, Pan Am believed that a new advanced-technology aircraft would be needed to break through into a new generation of subsonic jets. With the forecast of ever growing international business and pleasure travel and imminent over-crowding of the airways the new generation transport would have to be an airplane which could carry many passengers more per trip and be as fast as economically feasible. Higher productivity per airplane would be mandatory. Past experience proved that larger airplanes at higher speeds assured lower costs per passenger seat-mile and proportionately higher profits. Since airlanes were already somewhat congested by the 707—DC-8 types it was highly desirable that the newer, bigger, faster types should also be able to cruise at higher altitudes and fly above the existing airlanes.

The Pan Am staff was not remiss in failing to generate their own formal "cost-effectiveness" studies with elaborate and detailed trade-offs and options for their chief executive. Historically estimates and judgments as to the future had been made by Mr. Trippe alone at the roll-top desk that he had not discarded until he moved into the 46th floor corner suite of the Pan Am Building in 1963. Most of the senior members of the Pan Am staff had been with Mr. Trippe ever since he founded Pan Am in 1927. They and he had been living, in effect, in a "cost-effectiveness" atmosphere and in an optimistic and growing business day by day for almost forty years.

Mr. Trippe and his staff were intimately familiar with the basic dimensions of the air transport business. In 1950 there had been 4,500 transport airplanes in the airline fleets of the world. These 4,500 varied from DC-3s and even older aircraft to Constellations, DC-7s and Stratocruisers. Approaching 1970 air traffic would increase fourfold but 707s and DC-8s would be sufficiently highly productive to permit retiring great numbers of smaller, older propeller driven aircraft. By 1980 another two-hundred percent increase in air traffic was forecast. The airways could not accommodate anything like a two-hundred percent increase in aircraft. The requirement for a new transport about two-hundred percent more productive than the 707 and DC-8 was abundantly clear. And equally clear was the requirement for proportionate increases in passenger comforts and in overall safety.

Problem Solved By Advanced Power Plant. Happily the development of the even more powerful and efficient fan-jet engine presented another major advance or perhaps even a minor breakthrough in the evolution of the jet transport. Pan Am's original 707s were a highly successful breakthrough, largely attributed to the Pratt & Whitney JT3 engine, an adaptation of a military turbo-jet airplane engine to civil commercial use. All of the power of the JT3 came from the thrust or push of its rear jet exhausts. With the concept of the fan-jet engine, the JT3D, a further operational and economic step forward was made by Boeing's and Pan Am's 707-321, a big (189 economy-passenger) long range (intercontinental) fan-jet powered transport. The 707-321 with its JT3D engine was the final stage in the development of the 707 series.

Following the success of the JT3D, Pratt & Whitney, General Electric, and Rolls Royce pressed on with metallurgical development and a new concept of cooling the turbine-blades to permit the jet engines to operate at higher and more efficient temperatures. Pratt & Whitney produced a much larger fan with a by-pass ratio of 4.5 to 1. This big fan, inside its faired housing, acted as a propeller inside a cowling. This cowled or shrouded fan provided much more pull as a propeller than was provided by push from the jet exhausts.

With the combination of the higher operating temperatures and the high by-pass fan, the JT9 engine promised an improvement of 30% in the power provided per pound of fuel. A 30% increase in power plant performance was enough to assure a major advance in airplane performance and in airplane economics. Thus there was this potential for a great step forward with which to meet the economic requirement for a breakthrough into the '70s.

The C-5 Competition. In Seattle, in early 1965 Boeing was participating in fierce competition with Douglas and Lockheed for an Air Force contract to build the C-5—a military version of a much larger, higher performing jet transport that would break through into the '70s with lower ton-mile cost air transportation for huge quantities of military air cargo, important elements of which would be much larger than any current transports could carry.

It was clear to Pan Am from the beginning of the competition that the military requirement to carry massive outsize items of cargo from short, soft fields could not produce an aircraft with acceptably low operating costs to permit the economic carriage of passengers or normal air freight from the long smooth runways at the world's major terminals. It was equally clear that the advanced technology that was being applied to this big C-5 and the huge new engines also in competition could have some direct application and many beneficial side-effects on the advanced technology high performance civil commercial airplane that Pan Am wanted for a breakthrough into the '70s. Consequently it was clear to Pan Am that whichever company might win the C-5 contract, that company would have a marked advantage in converting its advanced military technological developments into civil commercial application.

It was natural therefore that Pan Am should establish contact with Boeing, Douglas, and Lockheed while they were in competition for the C-5. These contacts were established at the highest levels with all of these manufacturers. Mr. Trippe had conversations with Mr. Allen (Boeing), Mr. Donald Douglas, Sr. (Douglas), and Mr. Courtland Gross (Lockheed) and senior members of the Pan Am staff had more detailed discussions with their opposite numbers and normal points of contact in the staffs of the manufacturing companies.

On the day the Air Force contract was awarded, Mr. Frank Gledhill of Pan Am, who had just retired as Vice-President Technical Staff, was at the Douglas plant in California prepared to sign preliminary agreements for the production and purchase of a civil commercial version of the C-5. Gledhill's effort, of course, came to naught as the contract was given to Lockheed. The winner, Mr. Gross, was telephoned by Mr. Trippe within minutes after the announcement of the award of the C-5 contract. As he was being congratulated on winning the C-5 competition, he was also asked to begin negotiations for the production of a civil commercial version of the C-5 for initial purchase by Pan Am. Mr. Gross said that he would call back as soon as his staff felt that they had the military version well enough in hand to begin discussing a civil version. That day never came. For over five years Lockheed had its hands full indeed in trying to meet the demanding Air Force contract for which it had competed energetically and finally had won over Douglas.

Meanwhile Boeing also found its hands full with the production of growth models of the 707 and their highly successful and newly designed three-engine 727. In another area, competition was beginning to emerge from the French and the British through their planning for a supersonic transport, the Concorde. After being eliminated in the C-5 competition, Boeing's attention was focused directly on the civil commercial market for the '70s.

Stretch The 707? To make the optimum improvements on Boeing's highly successful 707, the Boeing and Pan Am staffs had a series of conferences over a variety of proposals. Further stretching of the fuselage was discussed in detail. It was finally concluded that a "stretched 707" would offer little improvement because the Pan Am development known as the 707-321 Intercontinental Model had already "stretched" the original 707-121 almost as much as the landing gear and general geometry would stand. Extending the long-tube-effect was another negative factor in further stretching the 707. And, of course, more and more weight in the same basic airframe produced more and more noise on take-off.

Pan Am was also in discussion with Douglas on improved DC-8s for the '70s. Since the DC-8 was a bit later than the 707, its design had not previously been stretched and, after considering double-decking and other more radical designs, Douglas elected to go the stretching route in improving its current model and the successful "Super DC-8" eventually evolved.

Double Deck The 707? After abandoning the concept of stretching, the Boeing - Pam Am staffs investigated in detail the practicability of double-decking the 707. It was concluded that the concept was technically feasible. Further growth of the 707-321 power plants (Pratt & Whitney's JT3D fan-jet series) could produce enough more power to operate a double decked 707. The concept of two circular 707 fuselages one on top of the other but faired into each other to form a fat figure-eight cross-section would produce almost twice the capacity of the current 707 at much less than twice the original cost or the operating cost. For a while, this concept looked promising.

Anticipating future air cargo demands for shipment in locked containers that could be moved from door to door by truck-airplane-truck (or rail or ship), Pan Am insisted from the beginning that its airplane of the '70s be designed for the carriage of cargo containers with an eight-foot by eight-foot cross-section and in lengths of ten, twenty, and even forty feet. Pan Am anticipated, correctly, that eight-by-eight containers with lengths varying by ten foot increments would eventually be accepted as a worldwide, land-sea-air standard.

The requirement for convertibility from passenger to cargo service led to discussions of convertible double-decked 707s that could carry eight-foot by eight-foot cargo containers on the lower deck and passengers on the upper, or cargo containers on both decks, or passengers on both decks. From these discussions emerged a whole series of new problems. All of the world's major passenger airports and terminals could handle a 707 load of passengers or a 707 load of cargo but none could (or perhaps ever should or would) handle these large loads simultaneously at the same terminal.

To land passengers at one terminal and then move the multi-million-dollar aircraft to another terminal to load or unload cargo would produce dead time on the ground that represented very large sums of money. Also some felt that there might be psychological problems in handling a full load of passengers on one deck with a full load of cargo of unknown nature on another; or even a load of passengers underneath another load of passengers. Simply moving passengers to the level of a second deck (about the level of the third floor of an ordinary building) at airports all over the world would itself be no small problem. One of the most difficult problems of all would be the emergency evacuation of that lofty top deck in the ninety seconds required before FAA would issue its certification of suitability for passenger carriage. No acceptable method of getting one hundred and seventy-five people down and out of that top deck in the same ninety seconds that the one hundred and seventy-five other people might be scrambling and "chuting" out of the lower-level had been devised. By mid 1965 the Boeing and Pan Am staffs just about gave up on either stretching or double-decking the great intercontinental 707-321.

Boeing's staff then had new discussions with the Pratt & Whitney staff, in which the Pan Am staff shortly joined. Pratt & Whitney had competed with General Electric for the production of radically new and advanced power plants for the C-5. Pratt & Whitney's entry was a large high by-pass ratio fan-jet with capability of eventual growth to about 50,000 pounds in thrust. Since General Electric had won the competition, Pratt & Whitney was in a position to modify and convert their entry to produce a big new-technology jet engine that would meet the civil commercial standards. Rolls Royce also had attractive plans for a new-technology high power jet engine. Pan Am discussed the possibility of producing 50,000 pounds take-off thrust with the Rolls staff in considerable detail. It was concluded that Rolls had the interest and the technical capability but there was serious doubt about their capability for extensive production and no doubt at all that a higher priority would be given by Rolls to their development of a different kind of new big engine for the British-French Supersonic Transport, the Concorde.

747 Conception. Eventually Pan Am, Boeing, and the engine manufacturers agreed that the time was ripe, the technology was adequately advanced, and the demands of world air commerce required a completely new high performance, high volume, low cost advanced technology air transport for the '70s. For the first years of the decade, the 747's capacity was expected to be somewhat greater than needed. For the later years, the performance might not be quite high enough. The target date was broadly "the seventies," as the target for the 707 had proved to be "the sixties."

The 747 was conceived.

After the give and take of a series of three-way staff conferences, there emerged the description of the new airplane that, at policy and executive levels, was judged to be possible of attainment although pushing the state-of-the-art in several respects as to air frame, the aircraft engine, and to some extent airline salesmanship, management, and ground handling equipment and techniques. It was clear to all parties at the outset that the cost of this project and the risks entailed in it represented a businessman's risk that, in event of failure, would wreck the Boeing Company and would bankrupt Pan American World Airways and any one of the three potential engine companies—Pratt & Whitney, General Electric, Rolls Royce. The detailed description of this machine and the terms under which this staggering venture would be launched were set forth as design objectives and company intentions in the letter signed by Mr. Allen and Mr. Trippe on December 22, 1965. Also a party to this project and the risks inherent in it was to be the one of the three competing engine companies which would shortly be selected by Boeing to power the 747.

Pan Am had had previous unhappy experiences wherein an aircraft manufacturer alibied failure to meet promised performance by claiming the engine manufacturer had failed to live up to its contract with Pan Am. When an airplane fails to meet a guaranteed speed, for example, no court could accept as valid any argument that the failure was caused either by inadequacies of engine thrust or anomalies or errors in the way in which the airplane manufacturer attached the engine to the airframe. Consequently Pan Am insisted in the case of the 747 that the contractual airplane performance guarantees would be solely by Boeing directly to Pan Am. Boeing was free to contract with whatever power plant manufacturer Boeing chose, but the final combined power plant and airframe performance would thus be Boeing's sole responsibility. Boeing selected the Pratt & Whitney JT9 as the engine to power the 747. Pan Am, of course, was not involved in any details of Boeing's contract or guarantees demanded by Boeing of Pratt & Whitney.

In this December 22nd statement of intent, Boeing estimated that the price of the 747 would be between $15,000,000.00 and $18,000,000.00 depending upon the final configuration of the air frame and the power plant. Because of the enormous costs of initiating the project, Pan Am was required to accept a prepayment scheme far more exacting than any previous experience. To initiate the project, Boeing demanded at the outset that Pan Am should agree to buy twenty-five 747s, pay two and a half percent of the cost of all twenty-five upon signing a definitive contract and, in increasing increments, pay fifty percent of the entire amount six months before the scheduled delivery of the first aircraft. This, by simple arithmetic and without consideration of interest or other charges, would commit Pan Am to pay Boeing up to a quarter of a billion dollars without one spare engine, without one spare part, and with no provision for essential specialized ground and terminal installations and equipment. Pan Am was to pay it before the Federal Aviation Administration could have completed the tests required to certify that the 747 could be used to fly passengers. That was the cost to Pan Am and the extent of its risk in this unprecedented speculative business enterprise.

In recognition of Pan Am's unique commitment to get the 747 program started, Boeing promised to refund to Pan Am seventy-five percent of any net profit before tax (in excess of five percent) that Boeing might accrue from sale of the first one hundred and fifty 747s. Pan Am attached little significance to this provision, judging that Boeing would be lucky indeed if they broke even on the first hundred and fifty—or even two hundred 747s.

The 1965 agreement laid out a time span of five years. The first two months of 1966 were set up for intensive Pan Am - Boeing staff conferences and agreements on basic characteristics and detailed specifications, after which Boeing would establish a firm base price and a definitive purchase agreement which in turn was to be signed by March 1, 1966.

Boeing then reserved five months to determine the likelihood of selling enough 747s to justify initiating manufacture. If firm orders for at least fifty 747s, including Pan Am's order for twenty-five, could not be assured, Boeing was free to cancel. If the program should proceed on schedule, Boeing planned to deliver to Pan Am for training and for outfitting two 747s without full FAA certification (747 NPs) in September and October 1969, the first of the fully certificated aircraft (747 Ns) to permit Pan Am to initiate scheduled operations in November 1969, and to have all twenty-three passenger models delivered by the end of May and in operation for the heavy summer season of 1970 and two cargo models for the late fall traffic that same year.

An unusual element of this basic agreement was the mutual intention that Boeing should exert best efforts to sell 747s to foreign flag carriers. Pan Am had had experience previously

December 1965–June 1967

when its initial 707s were barred from certain foreign airports on allegations that those foreign airports could not support such heavy, fast, new aircraft. These restrictions were lifted as quickly as the foreign government-owned or supported airlines based at such major key foreign terminals received their own 707s. Consequently Pan Am was not only willing but eager to assist Boeing's sales effort in key foreign countries. Pan Am even authorized Boeing to advise airlines' purchasing agents at major foreign bases, notably Japan and Italy, that Pan Am would consider helping train JAL and Alitalia crews in the operation of 747s.

Performance Objectives. In the initial agreement or the signed and accepted letter of intent, the 747 was to have a range of 5,100 miles with a full passenger load and at a speed of point nine Mach number (0.9M). With that loading it was to take off in 8000 feet on a warm day (84° F) on any present airport that could handle 707s or DC-8s, and then climb promptly to a 35,000 foot initial cruise altitude. It was to have passenger comfort and environment improved over the 707 and DC-8 level, stay within community noise levels, and be easily convertible for either passenger or cargo operation. Additionally this high performing airplane was to provide superior economics as compared with 707s or DC-8s at equivalent ranges.

With this airplane Pan Am would be able to take-off with three hundred and fifty to four hundred passengers from the shortest and weakest runways that were capable of supporting the current one hundred and eighty-five passenger 707-321, then climb to a traffic level above any current jets, and there enjoy a speed considerably higher than any competitor. Pan Am could then fly this full load on its longest heavily travelled international routes (Los Angeles–London or New York–Rio de Janeiro) in greater comfort than any competitor. Pan Am foresaw a great competitive advantage in being the first operator of the 747, realizing full well that its international competitors would follow its lead as rapidly as additional 747s could be built.

To guarantee being first with the 747, Pan Am insisted that the contract provide that the maximum practicable proportion of the initial production should be theirs. Pan Am could not assimilate all of the first twenty-five and Pan Am also wanted some of the first 747s to go to Air France, Alitalia, and Japan Air Lines. The initial letter agreement therefore guaranteed that Pan Am would receive the first two provisionally certificated 747-NPs for training (September and October 1969), the first five fully certificated 747 Ns for commercial operations (November and December 1969), five of the next ten 747 Ns (January and February 1970), five of the next ten (February and March 1970), five of the next ten (March and April 1970), and five of the next ten (April and May 1970). The two 747 NPs, after finishing their test function and some training, were scheduled to be returned to Boeing for refurbishment and such modification as the testing might have proved necessary and the redelivery to Pan Am as 747 Ns in the February and March quotas. In this manner Pan Am would have a clear lead over all competitors, foreign or domestic, but Boeing would have some early delivery positions to offer to other airlines which Pan Am hoped would be the vital foreign government-owned carriers.

Pan Am knew full well that there would be the normal disadvantage of being first with this new type of airplane. New airplanes and new engines have "bugs" that cannot be discovered or corrected except through heavy steady use in scheduled airline operation. The "bugs" in the airframe or the engine can be very serious indeed if safety is involved. "Bugs" can also be very expensive if schedule unreliability or operational irregularity are involved. Pan Am was also soberly aware of the likelihood of serious "bugs," since this would be the first time in American history that a totally new airframe and also a totally new engine had no breaking-in or proving ancestry in any military aircraft. The possibility of having all 747s grounded to correct some serious "bug" was not discounted.

A key element on which depended all of its attractive economic and operational features of the 747 and around which the engine was designed was the intention that the maximum gross weight would be 550,000 pounds. This key item, "Max Gross 550,000," later proved to be the basis for long, vigorous, and occasionally turbulent negotiations and renegotiations in the months and years that followed.

The Warm Glow of "Objectives" is Chilled by the Harsh Reality of "Specifications". The management, sales, and public relations echelons of both companies enjoyed a very merry Christmas after the December 22, 1965 agreement was signed. On both sides "visions of sugar plums danced through their heads."

After the Christmas euphoria wore off, the technical, engineering, business, and legal echelons on both sides entered their prescribed two months of negotiations to produce a firm contract with exact specifications, warranties, guarantees, and prices. The atmosphere grew grimmer and grimmer as the weeks progressed and attainable aerodynamic capabilities emerged.

It very soon became apparent on both sides that corporate discussion and problem-solving concerning the 747 was a far different matter than had been the case with the Stratocruiser and the 707 in years gone by. One reason was the sheer dimension of the 747 problems. Earlier problems had involved thousands and sometimes hundreds of thousands of dollars.

747 problems appeared to begin in the millions and go rapidly into multimillions. Both sides early recognized that items in the 707 program that might have been considered "nit-picking" were no longer "nits" when huge sums of money were concerned. "Nit-picking" in 747 dimensions was very serious, very big business.

Perhaps an equally important reason that 747 negotiations were far more exacting was the radical changes in the personnel supporting Mr. Allen and Mr. Trippe. Previously broad agreements entered into by Mr. Allen were translated into contracts by Messrs. Wellwood E. Beall, Edward C. Wells, and Maynard Pennell, all of whom had engineering training and backgrounds. Mr. Beall had left Boeing and was Donald Douglas' Senior Engineer. Mr. Thornton A. ("T") Wilson had been moved from his leading position in Boeing's huge Minuteman Missile Program into top management. Mr. John O. Yeasting, a former CPA and Boeing Comptroller, had taken over the Commercial Airplane Division in 1959. Mr. Yeasting was backed up and soon followed as Vice-President and General Manager of the Commercial Airplane Division by another Space and Missileman, Mr. Ernest H. (Tex) Boullioun. Mr. Wells was still Mr. Allen's topside aeronautical engineer but chose to avoid management and administrative matters. Mr. Pennell, then primarily involved with Boeing's Supersonic Transport venture, was the senior engineer directly under Mr. Boullioun and was only occasionally involved with the Boeing 747 negotiations. To the Pan Am team it appeared that the tone and spirit of the engineer had been superseded on the Boeing team by the drive of the successful space and missilemen and strongly influenced by the financial concern of the former Comptroller.

On the Pan Am side, Mr. Trippe had previously relied almost entirely on Vice-President Technical Staff Frank Gledhill for detailed negotiations and day-to-day contact with Boeing and other manufacturers. Mr. Gledhill had been with Mr. Trippe since the founding of Pan Am until he retired in early 1965. Mr. Gledhill was replaced by a retired General of the United States Air Force, Laurence S. Kuter. General Kuter had considerable air transport experience in the Air Force, where he had organized the Military Air Transport Service by the directed merger of the Air Force's Air Transport Command and the Navy's Naval Air Transport Service. MATS was the first integrated command in the new Department of Defense and General Kuter commanded it from its formation in 1948 through the Berlin Airlift and well into the Korean Airlift in 1951. Before that he had been the military member of the U.S.–U.K. Civil Aviation Conference at Bermuda. Following this he was seconded by the State Department to serve in civilian capacity as Chief of the U.S. Delegation to the International Civil Aviation Organization during its formative period 1946–48. Mr. Trippe brought General Kuter into Pan Am as a Vice-President after his retirement from the USAF in 1962 and had worked closely with him on technical matters. Where Mr. Trippe's relationship with Mr. Gledhill had been intimate and personal, with General Kuter it was close but organizational. By nature and background General Kuter called for more staff work and organizational functioning within his segment of the Pan Am staff than had been the practice with Mr. Gledhill.

As Vice-President Technical Staff, General Kuter established a primary team of negotiators representing the business, engineering, and legal interests of Pan Am with a second tier of staff experts who brought into play all the interests of the company.

Although the 747 was their major project, this same team was involved with a different set of Boeing negotiators concerned with Pan Am's order for fifteen U.S. Supersonic Transports. They were also involved with SUD Aviation in Paris and the British Aircraft Company, and to some extent the Bristol-Siddeley and later the Rolls-Royce Aircraft Engine authorities concerned with Pan Am's order for eight Concorde SSTs as well as the Dassault Company, which manufactured the Fan-Jet Falcon.

Under General Kuter as Vice-President Technical Staff, the primary negotiators were Vice-President Howard M. Blackwell, Purchasing; Vice-President Sanford B. Kauffman, Engineering; Chief Engineer John G. Borger; and Assistant Counsel Joseph A. Mannion. The leaders of the second tier of negotiators were Vice-President-Services, Harold L. Graham, from the Marketing Department and Chief Pilot-Technical Scott Flower from the Operations Department.

Hence, when Mr. Allen and Mr. Trippe met, they met as of old but discussed far greater dollar values than ever before. When the Boeing and Pan Am staffs met, new men met and the fact that their negotiations could make or break their companies was never taken lightly. They might appear to be "nit-pickers," but their "nits" were worth careful and precise picking.

In the process of developing the December 22nd agreement, Pan Am's Technical Staff had pressed for the maximum airplane performance which they judged that Boeing's best designers and engineers might attain and, in many cases of doubt, Pan Am demanded the optimum. On the Boeing side, before December 22nd the reservations and concern of the engineers and designers appeared to be less persuasive than the aspirations, hopes, and optimism of Mr. Allen and his sales, public relations, and comptroller staffs. As the manufacturer and the seller, Boeing obviously had to make promises sufficiently attractive to assure the early sale of from one hundred and fifty to two hundred big expensive 747s if Boeing was to break even.

Why Wide Body? The 747, of course, introduced the "wide body" to the air transport world where it was quickly copied in Douglas' DC-10 and Lockheed's 1011; and the British, French and the Russians were not far behind. It is extensively, effectively, and truly advertized as providing expansive room for passenger movement and a gracious, spacious change from the long narrow tube. The reason the 747 is some nineteen feet wide is, however, far more practical and mundane than the gracious provision of space in which passengers can stroll and clutter up the aisles. Very simply, Pan Am demanded that the 747 fuselage accommodate cargo containers eight feet by eight feet in cross-section. When the double decking concept was abandoned the eight-by-eight containers had to be placed side by side. To accommodate two abreast eight-by-eight containers in a circular fuselage, it must be some nineteen feet wide at shoulder level, with the external diameter of about twenty-one feet. Hence graciousness to passengers was the by-product of the demand for eight-by-eight cargo containers two abreast.

Why Second Story Cockpit? These same cargo containers are responsible for placing the flight deck and the flight crew in a cockpit on a top deck, high off the runway and not in the nose of the airplane as has always been the case with the 707 and DC-8. In the event a cargo laden 747 were to fail to clear an obstacle or otherwise be involved in an accident with a violent stop of forward motion, the momentum of 200,000 pounds of cargo in eight-by-eight containers would cause them to lurch forward and crush the crew unless the containers were restrained by exceedingly heavy structure. Hence the cockpit of the 747 is placed above the cargo load for the protection of the crew in case of an accident.

The Trade-Off Game. In the cold light of early January's engineering studies, the promises of performance that Boeing made in December became less and less attainable. It soon became apparent that all the power of Pratt & Whitney's proposed JT9D-1 engines just couldn't lift three hundred and fifty to four hundred passengers to 35,000 feet on a warm day and carry them 5,100 miles at Mach .9 in a 550,000 pound airplane. Some of these design objectives might be met but not all of them. The game of trade-offs began.

To carry three hundred and fifty to four hundred passengers 5,100 miles with the available power, great sacrifices would have to be made in speed and altitude and to carry the necessary fuel the airplane would have to weigh much more than 550,000 pounds at take-off. Another option would provide high speed and high altitude but with many fewer passengers and for distances far less than 5,100 miles.

To remedy their weight-power imbalance, Boeing demanded that Pratt & Whitney produce more power per engine without increase in engine weight, fuel consumption (also related to take-off weight), airport and community noise, and at no higher cost. Pratt & Whitney believed that they could accomplish some but not all of those things, but in phases during their three and six year cycles for the normally planned growth and development of their new engines. Pratt & Whitney, as well as Boeing, was also faced by the problem of producing a radically new fan-jet engine, without any proving or development by the Air Force. The Pratt & Whitney JT9D engine series was a wholly new concept—a high by-pass ratio fan-jet engine in which more propulsion was to be provided from the pull of the fan (a form of a shrouded propeller) than the push of the jet.

Time Schedule Begins to Slip. In January only one point was clearly undebatable from all viewpoints. Boeing could not produce a specification by January 24th that would even resemble the 747 airplane (and its appropriate engine) as it was described on December 22nd, less than five weeks earlier. Pan Am and Boeing had to agree to defer those terms in the agreement which required that Boeing produce the 'spec' by January 24th to give Pan Am five weeks of study and analysis and to reach a final and firm commitment with Boeing on or before March 1, 1966.

The requirement for a 747 freighter added to the complications in producing a 747 'spec'. From the beginning Pan Am had called for a cargo sister-ship (a 747-F) for the new passenger airplane. Some believed that a convertible 747 (a 747-C) which could carry passengers on one flight, or day, or season, and could then have seats, carpets and side-walls removed or converted to transport heavy cargo on demand would be technically feasible and economically desirable. 707-Cs and 727-Cs were in effective operation.

In the early months of 1966, engineers and negotiators had been fully involved in the passenger model of the 747. No details had been worked out on a 747F or 747C. It was obvious to all that the heavier floors and the loading equipment for a 747F would require an airplane even heavier than the passenger model 747 while a 747C would be even heavier still.

Pan Am suggested and Boeing agreed that the detailed contract should provide for twenty-three passenger aircraft and two freighters. Twenty-three was a number that would fit comfortably in Pan Am's summer schedules for 1970, and a requirement for two freighters at the end of the contract would reasonably fit into the fall and winter demand for air cargo capacity. Of perhaps more importance to Pan Am, the requirement to produce two 747Fs would assure that the Boeing engineers would give a marked second-priority attention to the design of a suitable cargo sister-ship, be it freighter or convertible.

Specifications were finally drawn up by Boeing which contained guarantees of performance approaching as closely as was believed possible to the objectives in what by now had become the "dream" of December 22nd, not too distant in the past to be memories that were painfully clear. On April 13, 1966 the firm contract, Purchase Order No. 189, for twenty-three passenger and two freighter models of the 747 was signed with varying degrees of reluctance on both sides. The Pan Am staff felt that Boeing should be able to do better than contractual guarantees for performance. The Boeing staff was not at all sure that they could do that well. A comparison of the performances envisioned by the letter of intent of December 22, 1965 and the guarantees in the contract of April 13, 1966 are tabulated below.

	DESIGN OBJECTIVES Agreement of 22 Dec. 1965	CONTRACT SPECIFICATIONS Purchase Order No. 189, 13 Apr. 1966
Capacity	350-400 Passengers and their baggage. Excess space for air cargo implied as was the practice with 707s and 727s.	370 Passengers and their baggage. No additional cargo, specified.
Range	5,100 Nautical Miles	At least 4,462 Nautical miles

December 1965–June 1967

Cruise Speed	Mach .90	Mach .877
Take-off	8,000 feet	9,900 feet
Initial Altitude	35,000 feet (above 707s and DC8s)	33,000 feet (along with 707s and DC8s)
Noise Levels	Not specified	13-117 PNDB
Weight	Take-off Gross Weight TOGW-550,000 lbs. approximate	TOGW not specified, but expected to be 655,000 lbs.
	Manufacturer's Empty Weight MEW-240,000 lbs. approx.	MEW-274,094 exact
Power	Boeing's option— estimated	Boeing chose Pratt & Whitney JT9D engine
	41,000 lbs. initial take-off thrust	41,000 lbs. initially
		44,000 lbs. in 3 years
		47,000 lbs. in 6 years

Changes in the Contract. Because of the pressure of time, a number of items had been left open for further study and appropriate modification of Purchase Agreement 189, as had been the practice with Pan Am's initial purchases of Boeing's 707s and 727s. Changes could be introduced by either party and the result would be a modification of 189 expressed by a dash number. Usually each successive dash number provided some added feature with an agreed change in weight and cost. Most of the changes were additions. Within the year the companies were discussing 189-7 and a related MEW of well over 300,000 pounds.

An example of a change introduced by Pan Am was the provision for a top deck cocktail lounge and the spiral stairway. While visiting Boeing's plywood 747 mock-up in early 1966, the Pan Am party noted considerable unused space under the fairing that smoothed out the top of the fuselage behind what would otherwise be a sharp bulge covering the cockpit crew. Pan Am remembered the great passenger appeal of the cocktail lounge below the main deck but reached by a spiral staircase in their post-war Boeing Stratocruisers. Pan Am proposed that the fairing be extended a bit farther back and the floor be strengthened to provide a cocktail lounge above the main deck to be reached by a spiral staircase. This change was engineered by Boeing. It added 4,420 pounds to the MEW and about $200,000 to the price. This cost was computed on the premise of a basic change in standard 747 design. The cost of providing it as an exclusive item in 747s for Pan Am alone would have been many times as great. At that cost Pan Am dropped any thought of restricting the use of the design.

Warm Interlude. A milestone in the 747 program and a happy interlude in Pan Am - Boeing staff discussions occurred in the middle of July 1966 when the City of Seattle celebrated the fiftieth anniversary of the Boeing Company. Seattle had a bronze medal cast "Honoring Aero Space Pioneers 1916—1966" and invited a large number of guests from all over the country to a civic banquet on July 15th. At the banquet Mr. Trippe made the speech which singled out Mr. Allen for the honors to the Boeing Company. In his response Mr. Allen referred to the 707 and 747 programs and implied that Mr. Trippe was more closely involved in their inception than normal in the relationship between manufacturer and customer.

On July 17th the guests and the press were invited for the first public visit to Boeing's finished, furnished and decorated plywood mock-up of the 747 interior. For the first time the wide-bodied concept with its double aisles and spaciousness was exposed to public comment. The comment was gratifying to the designers—the aerospace pioneers involved in the 747.

Stretch the 747? As initial engineering studies were refined, it became evident that elements of the airframe structure would not be strong enough without adding further weight. More detailed considerations of passenger comforts also developed requirements that would add weight to the design. As the airplane grew heavier and heavier, it became clear to all that engines with take-off thrust limited to 41,000 pounds lacked the power that was needed to make the 747 the desired "break-through into the '70s."

Pan Am, Boeing, and Pratt & Whitney had a happy history of successive phases of power plant development that justified successive "stretches" of the fuselage of the 707. When Pratt & Whitney's JT3 series of engines for Boeing's 707 reached its fan-jet JT3-D, its added power justified stretching the 707 fuselage by almost twenty linear feet and increasing its long range capacity from one hundred and forty to one hundred and eighty-seven economy passengers. In the case of the JT9D series of engines for the 747, there was reason to believe that the three hundred and seventy passenger airplane might be stretched to accommodate as many as four hundred and ninety passengers plus sixteen and a half tons of freight in the belly when the JT9D reached its three-year growth with 44,000 pounds of thrust and even greater stretching and capacity or a much higher performance when it reached 47,000 pounds after about six years.

Because of the mismatch of power and weight it was necessary to resize the airframe. It was decided to be bold and, in effect, to stretch the 747 at the outset. Pan Am and Boeing agreed that they could withstand some reduction in performance initially if a truly high performance 747 could be assured with the advent of the first stage of growth of the JT9D-1 engine. Both companies agreed that their combined pressure would result in greatly shortening the three-year period which Pratt & Whitney had maintained was required for that first stage of growth. The airframe was redesigned to accommodate four hundred and ninety economy passengers, and some related changes in the structure were redesigned proportionately.

By the end of March 1967, the MEW had grown from 274,094 pounds to 308,924 and there were no guarantees that it would not have to grow still more after testing.

By the end of this first year of the gestation of the 747, tempers were beginning to fray on the part of both parents, Pan Am and Boeing. The lower one went in the echelons of both staffs, the more precise became the unhappy data related to weight and power and the more frayed became the tempers.

As the design weight of the slowly incubating 747 grew and grew, much time was consumed and considerable heat was generated in debating responsibilities for this unending growth. Pan Am technicians argued with vigor and with some justice that Boeing design engineers had badly underestimated structural weights at the outset. Boeing debaters rebutted with vigor and with some justice that Pan Am kept adding frill after frill without regard for the heavier structure needed to support the frill or the added power entailed.

Eruption of June 9, 1967. On June 9, 1967 the power-weight problem was brought to a head by a letter under the official Boeing letterhead from Mr. J. B. Connelly, then Vice-President, Sales and soon to be promoted to Assistant General Manager, Commercial Aircraft Division, Boeing Aircraft Co., to General Laurence S. Kuter. Although this was a "Dear Larry" letter signed "Bruce," copies went to Pan Am's Vice-President-Purchasing, Howard M. Blackwell, who had many years experience as Pan Am's buyer, contract supervisor, and general businessman, as well as to Chief Engineer John G. Borger, an aeronautical engineer with worldwide stature as Pan Am's long-time expert in advancing the capabilities of transport aircraft and their engines.

In the letter of June 9th, Boeing implied that they would exceed MEW specified even in the latest of the agreed change orders, 189-7. Boeing implied that the 747 would be 13,000 pounds heavier than the nominal figure in the modified contract, 313,071 pounds. Boeing maintained that this was 5,000 pounds over the guarantee after applying their plus or minus two and a half percent tolerance. Missing a guaranteed 313,071 by 13,000 in terms of percentage on some business deals does not appear to be a crippling overrun. To Pan Am, a breach of contract consisting of an overrun of 13,000 pounds represented the loss of 13,000/220 = 58 international passengers on every long range flight. This in turn would represent the loss of perhaps $20,000 revenue per 747 flight. Such revenue from the last fifty-eight passengers that might have otherwise been taken aboard could reasonably be considered as very largely profit. On twenty-five 747s, potential losses of profit of that magnitude per day were not taken lightly at any echelon in Pan Am.

The Boeing letter than proposed to press on with the structural weight reduction program which had been underway for several weeks. This, of course, Pan Am applauded. However, Pan Am's engineers were convinced that further appreciable weight reductions, without jeopardy to safety, would entail extensive changes from steel and alloys to titanium at greatly added expense to Boeing. Pan Am forecast, accurately, that such would not happen.

Boeing also proposed that joint Pan Am - Boeing efforts might reduce the weight of each of the four hundred and ninety passenger seats in the economy configuration, the number, size, and weight of the seven galleys that would be needed to equal the ratios in the 707s, the extent of in-flight movies and sound entertainment, and other frills. Pan Am responded with assurances of continued close cooperation and collaboration.

Pan Am's letter in response to the June 9th declaration contained a clear and cold-eyed reminder that the full responsibility of meeting all agreed contract terms was the direct obligation of the Boeing Company. There was no doubt that Pan Am was convinced that it was Boeing, not Pan Am, that became pregnant when the 747 was conceived. Pan Am expected Boeing to make good on all commitments as to time of delivery and all elements of guaranteed airplane performance and other terms that were specified in the half billion dollar contract on which Pan Am had already paid some $12,000,000 and was then preparing to meet its next increment of $12,000,000 within the next few weeks.

To remedy the weight-power imbalance, the Boeing letter proposed still further redesign to carry the "stretch" to the optimum (which would make the airplane still heavier) and to put further pressure on Pratt & Whitney to increase engine power still more to meet increased weight. The weights envisioned were 710,000 TOGW with the accompanying MEW of about 321,000 pounds.

At this point the 747, which had been a 550,000 pound gleam in the eye at conception on December 22, 1965, after eighteen months gestation had grown to 710,000 pounds, with delivery still thirty months distant. No blueprints were needed to prove to both parents that growth at the rate of almost one thousand pounds per month would lead to disaster long before delivery.

The Boeing letter concluded with the proposal that the staffs again meet formally in August 1967 after Boeing had determined how much structural weight might be reduced. Pan Am accepted the invitation. The Pan Am staff did not expect that such a meeting would result in the most intense corporate clash in Boeing - Pan Am history.

The honeymoon was over!

CHAPTER 2

The Struggle For Performance Guarantees

June 1967–September 1968

Indignation in Pan Am. After the June 9th letter, several studies and separate investigations led to a major high level Pan Am - Boeing staff confrontation in mid-August 1967.

The Pan Am staff computed that the MEW would grow to over 331,000 pounds as a result of new requirements already appearing in the development program but not yet engineered in detail. Examples were the necessity to increase the weight of engine nacelles by some 1,080 pounds primarily to accommodate more silencing material which BOAC maintained would be required by the London Airport Authority, structural revisions related to heavier galleys, and several minor items. Some of these increases were chargeable to Pan Am changes and others, believed by Pan Am to be the heavier items, were chargeable to Boeing's revisions and correction.

Since the "overweight" problem was perhaps more accurately described as a problem of imbalance between growing weight and static power, Pan Am had several informal conferences with Pratt & Whitney. These conferences were largely for information since the terms of the basic Pan Am - Boeing contract very clearly specified that Boeing was fully responsible for the airplane and its power plant. Consequently Pan Am never inquired into Boeing's subcontract with Pratt & Whitney but requested from Pratt & Whitney full information on the development of the high by-pass JT9D power plant. In spite of Pratt & Whitney's subordination to Boeing in the Boeing - Pan Am contract, Pan Am's direct dealings with Pratt & Whitney became quite proper by virtue of Pan Am's direct contract with Pratt & Whitney for spare JT9D engines for some twenty-five 747s. This contract alone represented $20,000,000.

As a result of the Pan Am - Pratt & Whitney conferences, Pan Am concluded that the "overweight" airframes with the currently planned JT9D-1 engines would produce a 747 which could carry a full passenger load only 3400 nautical miles with no cargo or mail. This would produce an airplane suited to safe, reliable, year-round service in the New York—Paris route, but with inadequate range for New York—Rome. Additionally the initial cruise altitude of this 747 would be no higher than the 707 or DC-8, which would prohibit clearance at the higher altitude where the 747's higher speed could be used. It would require a runway 1000 feet longer than the 747 specifications, it would be noisier, and it would land six knots faster than the specification speed. This would introduce concerns of safety in blind-landing situations. All in all, the current 747—JT9D-1 combination would produce a passenger airplane which might be acceptable for very short and heavily travelled routes but which definitely would be inferior economically to the 707–321B on all of Pan Am's longer flights and which would be completely unacceptable as a freighter.

During this period, hundreds of people in New York, Hartford, and Seattle were concerned with the weight-power imbalance or the "overweight" problem of the developing 747 design. It was inevitable that the problem would leak to the aviation and business press. Even in the business press, speculations over these problems and rumors of the failure of the 747 program were beginning to appear.

Within the Pan Am staff it became known that this program, the joint effort of Pan Am and Boeing, was headed toward the production of a first group of airplanes which would be better suited to United or Eastern Airlines' short routes than for Pan Am's routes. Little solace was found in the knowledge that, further down the production line, engine power would be increased and long range operation would become feasible. The first group of "short range" 747s were, of course, the very airplanes that Pan Am was already paying for and was counting on so heavily to seize the market. Pan Am's great effort and heavy commitment seemed to be headed toward providing a windfall for the short range competitors and a heartbreak for Pan Am. The Pan Am staff never had the faintest intention of creating a breakthrough into the '70s, a world leading "first" and a great money maker for any of its many competitors. The reaction within the staff could quite reasonably be labelled "indignation."

The Boeing letter of June 9, 1967 concluded with the statement that Boeing would complete their further studies and be ready to present their conclusions on possible weight reductions and performance capabilities in August.

In preparing for the August conference and its inevitable staff confrontation, Pan Am considered several courses of action. Cancellation of the program and a law suit to recover the first prepayment of some $12,000,000 was never seriously considered. Technically Boeing had unequivocally stated that they could not meet some of the terms of the contract. Technically a suit for breach of contract appeared reasonable. Practically, however, no such action was seriously considered as the Pan Am - Boeing contract had been viewed from the beginning as an agreement far different from the ordinary business contract. As a practical fact, the specifications were little more than targets and the contract was little more than the means whereby the Pan Am staff could hold the Boeing staff's feet to the fire, if such should ever be necessary, to do their professional best to meet those difficult targets. In this respect the 747 contract was not unlike other contracts, civilian or military, for a new untried high-performance airplane. And furthermore, if Pan Am should sue and win, the results could either bankrupt Boeing (if the 747 program should be cancelled) or more likely would produce for Pan Am's shorter range competitors a 747 that should still be the world's best airplane for the shorter ranges, with no assurance of a good long range follow-on.

The courses of action which Pan Am considered were:

First, Pan Am could proceed with the present program and press for much faster growth in the power of the JT9D-1 engines. In favor of such action would be the receiving of the 747s on schedule, but receiving 747s which would be moneymakers only on the shorter routes. Against this course was the assurance that those 747s would be quickly rendered obsolete by the inevitable appearance of a better engine—an improved JT9D or even a new engine by General Electric or Rolls Royce.

A second course of action would be to delay the delivery of the 747s until a new and more powerful engine, which Pratt & Whitney would designate as a JT9D-5, could be produced and installed. Pan Am's power-plant experts estimated that the JT9D-5 could be in operation by December 1969, which would be three months after the originally contracted delivery date for the 747 with the JT9D-1. Pratt & Whitney's experts believed the delay would be ten months. Pan Am favored this course of action as it would produce initially a long range 747 with performance close to the original expectations. However, that delay in initial deliveries would cost Pan Am the interest on the $230,000,000 prepayment that was scheduled for completion in early '69. This interest would amount to very nearly $2,000,000 per month. The cost to Boeing of delaying the whole line was later estimated to be $400,000,000, which of course would have been prohibitive, and the cost to Pratt & Whitney of scrapping the JT9D-1 and changing to the JT9D-5 was out of the question.

A third course of action would be to avoid expensive delays by taking the initial airplanes with JT9D-1 engines and converting to JT9D-5s, or perhaps even bigger engines, as quickly as the engine makers could make the transition. This would keep Boeing's line moving, would not require Pratt & Whitney to scrap the JT9D-1, but would in this case also produce those very important "first" airplanes for Pan Am which would be money makers only on short ranges and would provide Pan Am's competitors whose delivery positions were farther down the production line with improved 747s which would be far superior on the longest routes.

A final proposal consisted of adjustment among the three basic courses. Pan Am believed that a highly desirable element of such adjustment would be an agreement by Boeing to take back in trade at book value the initial short range airplanes as quickly as the long range JT9D-5 powered aircraft became available.

Confrontation Number One. Not wanting to wait until August to begin resolving the problems set forth in the June 9th letter, General Kuter urged Mr. Yeasting, then the General Manager of Boeing's Commercial Aircraft Division, to speed up the process. Mr. Yeasting agreed that the staffs might discuss solutions on a tentative basis in conference at the Boeing plant in Seattle at 0900 Friday July 14, 1967. That proved to be the opening round of intense staff controversies. This controversy was active in varying stages of heat until the fifteenth modification of the basic contract (189-15) was signed fourteen months later. Involved were the working and negotiating staffs of both companies and, from time to time, Mr. Trippe and Mr. Allen in private and in team discussion.

Round One. Present on July 14th in the Boeing plant were: for Pan Am, General Kuter, the Vice-President - Technical Staff and his assistants Mr. Sandford Kauffman, Vice-President - Engineering, Mr. Howard Blackwell, Vice-President - Purchasing, and Mr. John Borger, Chief Engineer; and for Boeing, Mr. John Yeasting and his principal assistants, Mr. E. H. ("Tex") Boullioun, Mr. Ed Wells, long-time top-level engineer, Mr. Maynard Pennell, temporarily the 747 Project Engineer, Mr. Malcolm Stamper, 747 Factory Manager, Mr. Tom Spalding, Director of Contractual Administration, Mr. Snyder, his legal assistant, and Mr. Carl Munson, Boeing's salesman on the Pan Am account.

General Kuter opened the conference with a recital of the shortcomings of the current 747; a contrast between initial objectives, contractual specification, and current computations and forecasts; and a conclusion that the current 747 was no improvement over the 707 at the longer ranges, with the decision that the "current 747 was not acceptable to Pan Am." Mr. Yeasting responded with more optimistic economic data based on short-range operation of the 747. He then asked for a recess while the Boeing staff considered the position Pan Am had presented.

After visiting the engineering mock-up of the new 747 at Boeing's Everett plant and observing that 747 production was proceeding approximately on schedule, the Pan Am staff was invited back to Boeing's main offices at Renton to hear the Boeing reaction to the Pan Am position. There followed a resume of the current situation which in general matched the Connelly-Kuter letter of June 9th. A vigorous weight reduction program had been initiated by Boeing's engineers. Mr. Yeasting explained that Boeing also was considering several alternative courses of remedial action including program changes based on Pratt & Whitney's JT9D-5 engine, staying with the current program, adjusting the current program for more rapid engine growth, and other possibilities. All of Boeing's courses of action were based upon the provision of more power, none were premised on any major reductions in weight. Boeing concluded that Pratt & Whitney would have to produce more data and, pending its receipt, Boeing proposed an adjournment of the discussion with Pan Am until July 28th.

Pan Am urgently pressed for decisions in less than two weeks, arguing that six weeks had already elapsed since the overweights were known and that two more would result in a delay in decision by two full months. Since Pratt & Whitney had said that waiting for the JT9D-5 might delay the program as much as ten months, these two months could result in a full year's hiatus. Finally Boeing agreed to wire and telephone Hartford and have further staff conversations on Monday or Tuesday 17-18 July. The Pan Am staff stayed in Seattle, where they noted the Boeing staff at work in their offices and plants with no Saturday or Sunday off.

In the early hours of Monday July 19th in Seattle, Pan Am (John Borger) called Pratt & Whitney (Art Smith, the Executive Vice-President) to stress the urgency of data on increased engine power. Still in the early hours in Seattle, Pan Am (General Kuter) talked to the New York headquarters (Mr. Harold E. Gray, the President) to report the status of discussion and the general observation that the business and financial approach of Mr. Yeasting and Boeing's finance and legal staffs was prevailing over the requirement to improve airplane performance, which was in the province of Mr. Wells,

Mr. Pennell, and their aeronautical engineers. The result was an appearance of much less urgency and concern by the Boeing staff over the 747's performance than was felt by the Pan Am staff.

At noon the Pan Am group was invited to a luncheon conference with the Boeing party. Present were most of Boeing's negotiators. A place was set for Mr. Yeasting, who never arrived. Mr. Bouillioun said that he was in detailed discussion with Mr. Allen.

During and following the luncheon, Mr. Boullioun outlined several alternative 747 programs on which he had competitive Boeing teams at work. The alternatives included: (1) adhering to the current program but placing still more emphasis on weight reduction by Boeing and on power increases by Pratt & Whitney, (2) deferring until the JT9D-5 engine could be produced, (3) changing to a five or six engine 747 by using four of the current JT9D-1 engines hung under the wings and adding one or two of the smaller JT3-D engines (which were performing so well in the 707s) in the tail of the 747 or alongside the rear fuselage, or (4) to cut off the current 747 after two hundred airplanes, which was still believed to be the break-even number, and then produce a much improved 747B with much bigger engines.

Pan Am responded that several of those alternatives had been considered within the airline but none appeared to offer much promise except holding for the JT9D-5, which Pan Am believed would be very costly. Pan Am, however, expressed pleasure over the energy which Boeing was then devoting to find a solution. Mr. Boullioun believed that he might have more data by Wednesday July 19th. In reporting back by telephone to the President of Pan Am, General Kuter expressed the belief that the continued presence of Pan Am's high level team over the week-end had contributed to Boeing's new sense of urgency, and President Gray agreed that the team should stay on in Seattle.

During these days of staff skirmishes, the Pan Am "command post" was a living room at a corner of the eighth floor of the Olympic Hotel in Seattle. General Kuter and Mr. Kauffman had bedrooms adjoining this corner room and the other members of the party were scattered throughout the hotel. The Command Post was busy day and night and the telephone was kept very busy with calls to the Pan Am Building in New York, Pratt & Whitney in Hartford, and the many Boeing offices and plants in Seattle, Renton, and Everett. Pan Am had maintained an office of inspectors and contract administrators in Seattle under Mr. Robert B. Blake, who, naturally, was in and out of the command post frequently along with other Pan Am visiting technicians and officials who were in liaison with many elements of the Boeing Company.

On July 18th Boeing was not prepared to meet with Pan Am, but a breakfast conference was scheduled for July 19th between the parties who had opened this series on the 14th. Initially Boeing outlined and forecast success in its vigorous and competitive weight reduction campaign. Then and over the balance of the morning Boeing presented four alternative programs which had been laid out in chart form over the periods from 1968 to 1978.

Program A was based on Pratt & Whitney's new proposal to replace the initial JT9D-1 engines, which were expected to produce 42,000 pounds take-off thrust, with a slightly modified engine to be identified as a JT9D-3. This engine would be expected to produce 43,500 pounds by mid-1970 and to grow to produce 44,000 pounds in the second half of 1971 and finally to 47,000 pounds in 1974 or 1975.

Program B would await the JT9D-5 engine to be designed

to produce 44,400 pounds of thrust initially, 46,000 pounds in late 1972, and 49,500 pounds eventually, perhaps in mid-1975. This program could entail delays of as much as a full year in Boeing's opinion.

Program C would be based on Program A but include a new 747B in early 1973 with a 53,000 pound thrust engine which would grow to 56,000 pounds in 1975.

Program D also was based on Program A but with two smaller engines (707 type) or one additional JT9D-1 in the tail in early 1973.

Pan Am observed that none of the programs except "B" could produce a 747 meeting specifications until 1974 and argued that the JT9D-5 powered model could be produced with less than a whole year's delay. Pan Am's Chief Engineer Borger proposed ways to reduce the delay to a minimum of three or a maximum of six and a half months. Boullioun countered that Boeing would have produced seventy airframes by the time the JT9D-5 engines could be in production. He then departed, presumably to report to Mr. Allen.

Boeing announced that a Pratt & Whitney team was enroute to Seattle to establish firm dates and prices on these several programs and implied that Friday July 28th was the earliest date by which further progress might be expected. Pan Am pressed that this added delay be shortened and that the next meeting be scheduled no later than July 26th.

After a telephone report back to the Pan Am Building, the team packed up, cleared the hotel and, on the transcontinental flight back to New York, around a table in the lounge of a United Airline DC-8, outlined a report to the President on Round One and outlined further preparation for Round Two.

Whether Round One was win, lose, or draw was never quite decided. Pan Am had not agreed to accept a degraded 747.

Boeing had not agreed to produce one up to specification. Perhaps "draw" was the decision to Round One.

In preparing for the next conference on July 28th, or hopefully the 26th, the Pan Am staff drew up a series of economic and operational tables which were based on the 747 at its currently estimated weight and with engine power that might be provided by the JT9D-1, its growth version, and a still larger engine, a JT9D-7 which might power a 747B. It was again concluded that the 747 would be under-powered with the JT9D-1 even at its first stage of growth after three years of operation. Pan Am could not afford the economic handicap which would result from three years of operation at greatly reduced loads on its longer routes.

Further reductions in airframe weight would require replacing most of the steel and alloys in the airframe with titanium, which would mean great increases in cost and further delay. The use of new exotic metals could not be relied upon because they were only beginning to emerge from metallurgical research and development.

There being no apparent alternative, it was concluded that the Pan Am staff should use whatever contractual pressure it would generate to produce a JT9D-5 powered 747 at the outset and also have the airframe strengthened where necessary to justify the Federal Aviation Administration certification at 710,000 pounds or more so that the 747 could carry the heavier loads that could be lifted by the JT9D-5.

Pan Am computed that the extra costs of JT9D-5 engines ($100,000 to $200,000 per engine) and the added cost of operation and maintainance for the higher power engines ($75,000 per year) would be far less than the return from a ten to twenty percent increase in payload. In addition substantial economic benefits would result from the higher power JT9D-5

June 1967–September 1968 41

by gaining flexibility in scheduling long and short legs on round-the-world services, higher initial cruise altitude, less take-off community noise, and the overall advantage of average operations at less than full engine power.

As a result of frequent Pratt & Whitney/Pan Am staff contact, it was concluded that Boeing was likely to propose converting to an intermediate engine, the JT9D-3, for initial equipment if Pratt & Whitney could assure delivery early enough to permit Boeing to meet its contractual delivery dates. While a great deal better than the JT9D-1, the -3 version would result in 747 performance that would still fall somewhat short of specification guarantees.

Consequently the staff urged President Gray to convince the Chairman of the Board, Mr. Trippe, who was out of the country on other business, to add his influence to Round Two by telephoning Mr. Jack Horner or Bill Gwinn of United Aircraft and Pratt & Whitney, as well as Mr. Allen of Boeing, to press for the earliest production of the biggest practicable engine (which was judged to be the JT9D-5) at the lowest increase of cost.

Round Two, Blow by Blow. On Monday and Tuesday, July 24th and 25th, the Boeing staff telephoned to say that they were working hard with the Pratt & Whitney party but would not be prepared to meet the Pan Am staff on Wednesday, probably not on Thursday, but most likely could meet on Friday as they had forecast a week earlier. In response General Kuter told Mr. Connelly that Pan Am regarded delays so expensive and the 747—JT9D-5 program so important that the Pan Am team would come to Seattle on the chance that the day and night work presumably underway between Pratt & Whitney and Boeing could produce results worth discussion on Wednesday. On Tuesday night, July 25th, the same

Pan Am team (Kuter, Kauffman, Blackwell, and Borger) moved back into the same command post in the eighth floor corner of the Olympic Hotel.

Boeing politely recognized the Pan Am pressure indicated by the early arrival of the Pan Am team and announced that they would not be prepared to talk on Wednesday. Boeing also was not averse to applying pressure, as evidenced by their announcement of United Air Line's order for thirteen additional 747s, which appeared under great front-page headlines in the Seattle evening paper on the night of the arrival of the Pan Am team. The story said that the order was signed in May of 1967. Although United's routes were much shorter than Pan Am's, it was nevertheless clear that not all of Boeing's customers were as hard nosed as Pan Am about long range, heavy load performance and had signed up under less demanding terms.

On Wednesday, by telephone, the principals (Trippe, Allen, and Gwinn) reentered the negotiations. President Gray, by telephone from New York, told the Pan Am team that Mr. Trippe had talked to Mr. Gwinn and concluded that even the JT9D-5 engine was no breakthrough into exciting performance and Mr. Trippe believed that Pan Am should press at the outset for the biggest engine of all, the JT9D-7. This was no surprise to the Pan Am staff, because Mr. Trippe habitually had demanded that his engines and airplanes always be the biggest and best. It was also no surprise that Mr. Trippe did not believe, or chose to ignore, that the JT9D-7 engine had to have a bigger fan, a bigger case, a bigger nacelle, and consequently would require major structural redesign of the 747 wing, engine mounting, and landing gear. The Pan Am staff decided to accept its instructions without argument and plug for the JT9D-7 but accept the -5 as a first line of retreat.

The Boeing - Pan Am principals joined the fray to the marked advantage of the Pan Am team. After his telephone conversation with Seattle, Mr. Trippe reported that Mr. Allen stated unequivocally that Boeing would meet the terms of the contract. When Mr. Allen said that a six months deferment of the delivery would cost Boeing $400,000,000, Mr. Trippe had said the current 747 was a far cry from adequate performance and Pan Am needed a better long-range load carrier with a gross weight "like 717,500 pounds" and a matching engine "like the JT9D-7."

Boeing set 1100 hours Friday morning July 28th for the major confrontation. Present were the same teams that had met on July 14th.

Mr. Yeasting opened the conference with the statement that Boeing's position had been reviewed by Mr. Allen, who had talked to Mr. Trippe. He gave no indication of what Mr. Trippe's reaction might have been. He and his engineers then reviewed programs A, B, C, D, and a new E that referred to a distant future 747 grossing something "like 717,500 pounds" with an engine "like the JT9D-7."

He concluded that a 710,000 pound 747 with the JT9D-3 would be better than the 680,000 pound-JT9D-1 currently planned and that any advantages of waiting for a JT9D-5 were rendered impracticable by the cost to Boeing of six months delay. He went into considerable detail to show why the delay would last at least six months and why it would cost Boeing between 250 and 450 million dollars. He referred to unknown problems with Boeing's other twenty-six customers and rejected any further consideration of any substantial delays in the program. He presented Boeing's position in six parts:

(1) Boeing would proceed on the current 747 program.

(2) Boeing would continue their weight reduction program.

(3) Boeing would proceed to have the 747 certificated by the FAA for 680,000 pound take-off and to have that limit extended to 710,000 pounds by 1 June 1970 at no added cost but with added airframe weight up to 1000 pounds if necessary.

(4) Boeing meanwhile would secure Pratt & Whitney's "best efforts" to deliver the JT9D-3 engine in lieu of the JT9D-1 as initial equipment. Boeing was confident that the JT9D-3 could surely be produced in sufficient quantity to begin equipping the fortieth 747 in the production line so that no more than the initial thirty-nine 747s would have to be equipped with the JT9D-1. Boeing then maintained that the thirty-nine initial 747s equipped with the JT9D-1s could be converted to JT9D-3s in the summer of 1970 at a cost of $200,000 per engine plus labor. Of the initial thirty-nine 747s, twenty would be Pan Am's. Boeing did not mention that their conversion to JT9D-3 engines would take the planes out of operation for long periods during the peak of the 1970 travel season.

(5) Boeing would renegotiate the contact with new performance guarantees (all of which, presumably, would provide for lower performance than the current contract).

(6) Boeing would be unable to discuss the two freighters provided for in the Pan Am contract for two or three months.

To assure his understanding that Boeing was proposing to renegotiate a contract whereby Pan Am would pay more for a poorer performing airplane, General Kuter asked that several items in the Boeing presentation be restated. The understanding was confirmed. General Kuter asked for an adjournment for caucus and resumption later in the afternoon. Both parties moved to the Boeing staff dining room for a very strained and tense luncheon.

After luncheon, separate caucuses, and Pan Am's telephone conference with President Gray, the teams reconvened at 1545 July 28th for a brief but firm statement of impasse.

General Kuter opened with reference to Mr. Yeasting's statement that Mr. Allen and Mr. Trippe had been in telephone conversation and his understanding that Mr. Allen had been firm and clear in his statement that Boeing would live up to the contract. This good news did not appear to be at all in harmony with the Connelly letter of June 9th, the discussions following, or anything in this day's discussions.

After an eloquent pause, Mr. Yeasting asked to have Mr. Allen's statement repeated. This was done slowly as all members of the Boeing party were writing it down.

As to the current 747 program, Pan Am concluded that it was unacceptable from a revenue viewpoint (restricted payload and range) and unacceptable from an operational viewpoint (take-off, climb, cruise altitude, noise, and approach speed).

General Kuter closed with the statement that he had neither the intent nor the authority to renegotiate the existing contract, and particularly to accept Boeing's proposal to provide a poorer airplane at higher cost.

After this conclusion, Mr. Yeasting repeated the Boeing plan to proceed with the current 747 program and the meeting adjourned at the lowest point of many years of corporate cooperation, collaboration, and business relationship.

Round Two surely provided no victories. Both sides demonstrated grim determination and a hard hitting approach. Each landed haymakers but neither was floored, and another round was coming up.

On Saturday July 29th, President Gray was in his office at 1800 hours awaiting the return of the Pan Am team after Round Two in Seattle.

Boeing Changes Line Up. After reviewing the Seattle session, it was determined that little would come of further Allen-Trippe conversations other than pointing out the fact that Mr. Yeasting and staff were presenting positions far afield from Mr. Allen's assurance that Boeing could meet the specifications in the contract. Mr. Yeasting was shortly promoted to a Senior Vice-Presidency in the top Boeing hierarchy and Mr. E. H. Boullioun replaced him as Vice-President and General Manager of the Commercial Airplane Division and became the senior negotiator in the 747 program. A new atmosphere was immediately apparent. The Pan Am team felt a marked change from a cautious and conservative background of accounting and comptrollership to a driving progressive background of field operations, engineering, and production in aerospace and missiles.

Largely to keep negotiations from stalling at bottom deadcenter, a message was dispatched on Monday July 31st from Gray to Yeasting asking for specifics in the guarantees he had proposed renegotiating. There resulted a flood of telegraphic negotiations over company-leased TWX lines.

Six Foot Telegram. The response bore a time-date mark of 0255 August 1. It was obvious that the Boeing staff was at work. This response was in the form of a TWX which was six feet and nine inches long. It spelled out in detail the reductions in performances which they could guarantee in the 680,000 pound JT9D-1 powered 747 which had been outlined during the July 28th confrontation. Mr. Gray responded immediately that such an airplane would be unacceptable economically and unacceptable operationally. These familiar words now had formal corporate sanction on the

June 1967–September 1968

written record. Mr. Gray also telephoned and asked for an immediate response, inserting a new note of urgency by his estimates that delays in the 747 program would cost Pan Am a million dollars a day in revenue.

The next message was dispatched from Renton at 2115 hours PDST August 3rd and on careful measurement it was ten feet long and was referred to from then on as the "Ten Foot TWX."

Ten Foot Telegram. The Ten Foot TWX opened with the substantial concession that the JT9D-1 was now dead and Pan Am's first 747s would be equipped with the JT9D-3. The message included performance guarantees under four conditions: TOGW 680,000 pounds and 710,000 pounds with take-off thrust at 43,500 pounds (JT9D-3 initial) and 45,500 pounds at the first stage of growth. At 45,500 pounds of thrust, the 747 was a very attractive airplane but, of course, that performance could not be attained until late '71 or early '72. The Ten Foot TWX concluded by repeating the assertion made in conference that Pan Am would have to make additional payments for the more powerful JT9D-3 engine.

President Gray telephoned promptly to express his gratification that a better engine than the JT9D-1 would be installed in the initial airplanes and that the resultant performance would come closer to the existing contractual specification. He then stated slowly and firmly that he could not justify accepting any 747 if he was expected to pay more for an engine which still would fall short of meeting specification performance or to accept any airplane with a faster landing speed than the current 707.

Part of Boeing's campaign to reduce weight had been to change from the heavy triple-slotted landing flap which assured a slow landing speed to a conventional double-slotted flap which produced a landing speed several knots faster.

Mr. Gray also said that he could not consider accepting passenger models until he was sure that there would be an efficient freighter as a "sister ship." He further observed that newer and better engines should be available to render Pan Am's initial 747s obsolete by 1973 and there should be some plan for Boeing to take the original 747s back in trade for advanced models.

The next day Mr. Yeasting called General Kuter and further conceded that the JT9D-3 engines would be provided to Pan Am at no extra cost. This concession was confirmed by TWX forthwith. General Kuter observed that such action seemed to be reasonable but several items required an answer to justify acceptance by Mr. Gray of either the passenger or the freight model. Mr. Yeasting agreed that further word was needed from Boeing.

The next day Mr. Trippe left for Seattle with Mrs. Trippe to visit the Boeing plant and thereafter to spend a week or ten days fishing in Alaskan waters from the Boeing cruiser with Mr. and Mrs. Allen. General Kuter reviewed for Mr. Trippe's information the status of the negotiations with Boeing and discussed a change in plan which might be considered by Boeing. The plan involved cancelling the contract for twenty-five 747s and substituting one for thirty. The first ten would be those airplanes now scheduled for first delivery, with JT9D-3 engines and triple-slotted flaps, all in accord with the existing contract, the Ten Foot TWX, and subsequent agreements. The second ten would be the first batch of an improved 747 (the 747B) with much more powerful engines "like the JT9D-7 or better" and a bigger payload. Delivery should begin in late '71. The third ten would follow on in early 1973. Pan Am should also have the option to return the first ten 747s at seventy-five percent of their cost.

Mr. Trippe asked to have this plan in writing and also asked to have its contents restricted in Pan Am and unknown in the Boeing plant. Six copies, simply entitled "Plan A" on plain paper with no letterhead, were prepared and Mr. Trippe took two with him as he left for Seattle.

Whether or not this plan was ever discussed during Mr. Trippe's several visits in the plant and many days with Mr. Allen was never stated, nor was this at all unusual in Mr. Trippe's way of dealing with his staff. His own negotiations were never written, always oral, and under circumstances where there were no observers or staff members to make notes or to report. His ability to disclaim in private what his staff had proposed in conferences was a negotiating weapon he cherished. He reserved the right, and frequently exercised it, to redirect the subjects under discussion into new and unexpected directions.

While it was unknown whether "Plan A" was proposed, it became quite clear that one element was most certainly presented—a spectacular follow-on for the 747 in late 1971—Mr. Trippe's 747B. This type diversion was also quite in keeping with Mr. Trippe's interests and practices. Although his company and Boeing were at loggerheads over the development and production of the initial 747, he was already building fires under Boeing and Pratt & Whitney chief executives to lay out a follow-on with vastly improved capabilities.

Bigger and Better. Mr. Trippe called back from Seattle to express Mr. Allen's concern that Pratt & Whitney would not be at all anxious to build a fifty or sixty thousand pound thrust engine only two years after producing their forty to fifty thousand pound JT9D-1 and -3. Nevertheless the Pan Am staff was directed to get to Hartford and "convince those executive-level Pratt & Whitney people to produce such an engine one year and nine months after the JT9D-3."

Accordingly an appointment was sought urgently with Mr. Art Smith, Pratt & Whitney President. Mr. Smith understood Mr. Trippe's pressures, asked for one day for preparation, then scheduled a staff meeting with the Pan Am party for Wednesday morning August 9th. It was concluded that an engine delivering 60,000 pounds take-off thrust, with constant 14,000 pounds cruise thrust, and weighing about 13,000 pounds would be needed to produce the 747 performance Mr. Trippe wanted. It was also concluded that the state-of-the-art was adequate to produce such an engine in one year and nine months. Finally, Mr. Smith offered the "ball park" estimate that the cost to Pratt & Whitney of producing that powerful an engine in that short a time would be $250,000,000. At a luncheon with Mr. Jack Horner, Bill Gwinn, and other top United Aircraft officials, such a program was reviewed, discussed, and "costed" on the back of Mr. Horner's menu. By the time for dessert the cost was $350,000,000. General Kuter commented that it was unfortunate that the Pan Am party had stayed for that very expensive dessert. None of these gentlemen believed that these exceedingly high costs would kill the interest in a 60,000 pound engine for Mr. Trippe's 747B. They too had known Mr. Trippe for years.

Another phone call from Mr. Yeasting to General Kuter on August 10th, possibly prompted by the Trippe visit in Seattle, promised another concession in the 747 controversy by announcing that the first airplanes would have the triple-slotted flaps (and accompanying lower landing speed) restored at no extra cost and at no increase in weight. General Kuter noted that this act removed one of President Gray's objections to accepting any 747s, but several objections still remained. Another TWX confirmed this concession and recognized further problems to solve.

On August 14th, Mr. Trippe returned to New York from his conference with Boeing and the fishing trip with the Allens. He had several enthusiastic conferences with General Kuter and the engineers and initiated lengthy telephone conversations back with Mr. Allen. He spelled out in detail the characteristics of the 747Bs which he wanted in the fall of '71. These included space to carry about 500 economy passengers and their baggage and also twenty tons of cargo and mail on Pan Am's longest routes or one hundred tons tare of freight in the freighter version for at least the New York-Paris routes. The airplane was to climb to and cruise initially at 37,000 feet and be pressurized for 45,000 to assure flying above all other traffic and to have better take-off, slower landing speed, and less noise than current 707s or DC-8s. Mr. Trippe urged Mr. Allen to direct his senior designer, Mr. Ed Wells, to get in touch with General Kuter the next day to initiate the design and development of such an airplane without delay.

Some of the Trippe enthusiasm for a giant leap ahead to the 747B while the basic 747 was still in doubt was transmitted to the Boeing engineers but not enough to lead them again into unrealistic promises. Although the Trippe enthusiasm cost many thousand man-hours work by Boeing engineers and the negotiation teams, this effort was by no means all waste. There was some fall-out from the engineering studies to the benefit of the original 747, some results benefited the growth plans for the 747 and its engines, and all of the effort underscored Pan Am's dissatisfaction with the performance of the 747, which probably was Mr. Trippe's unacknowledged objective at the outset.

After many Wells-Kuter telephone conferences, it was concluded that the 30th of September was the earliest date by which the engineers could produce data worthy of joint discussions, Mr. Trippe's impatience notwithstanding. At that time a party of four Boeing engineers came to the Pan Am headquarters and presented a series of conclusions. Basically the engineers determined that performance such as Mr. Trippe was demanding (particularly an initial cruise altitude of 37,000 feet) simply could not be obtained with the current and highly engineered wing of the 747 or from any engines with the outside dimensions of the JT9D series. A new and bigger wing and airframe and a new engine would be required. Their "ball park" estimates were that about thirty feet additional wing span, about 52,000 pounds take-off thrust, and an overall airframe weighing about 850,000 pounds would be required. It was apparent to all at staff level that such an airplane could not conceivably be produced in the fall of 1971. The Pan Am pressure was nevertheless still exerted for the greatest attainable improvement for late '71. Without enthusiasm, the Boeing staff moved to Hartford for further discussions of attainable improvements in power by Pratt & Whitney, and both airframe and power plant engineers moved back to Seattle on September 5th for further intense joint effort to meet as many as possible of the Trippe requirements.

Meanwhile on September 1, 1967 a five percent payment on Purchase Order 189 was due from Pan Am. That payment of $29,205,875 was made on September 1st and transmitted in a Kuter to Connelly note which very pointedly stated that Pan Am was living up to its terms of the Pan Am - Boeing contract to the letter. The note also made it clear that the payment was presented without surrendering any rights or claims under the contract although the payment followed Boeing's June 9th letter and the joint staff discussions of the likelihood that performance guarantees in the contract would not be met. The Pan Am letter and the payment were promptly and officially acknowledged at staff level. About a month later, in personal conversation, Mr. Allen expressed to Mr. Trippe considerable umbrage over the substance of the Pan Am Letter. The needle had quite obviously been felt at the highest levels in Boeing. Mr. Trippe did not withdraw the needle. Similar letters were written on each of the subsequent payments. The Pan Am staff was determined to miss no opportunities to apply all the pressure available for the optimum performance of the 747. The Boeing staff very clearly understood that position.

A side opportunity to apply more pressure was the fact that Pan Am was due to order more 707s for delivery in late '68 and early '69. Pan Am had long held an option for nineteen additional intercontinental 707-321Bs. These aircraft would be needed to meet the demands of increasing travel before the 747s could be put into operation and thereafter for use on the less heavily travelled routes following the delivery of the 747s.

The staff drafted several orders for nineteen aircraft. Draft orders were set up as cancellable unless several conditions were met in the 747 negotiations. These conditions leaked to the Boeing staff. Since the option for nineteen 707-321Bs represented a sale well over $100,000,000, even rumored conditional considerations were not taken lightly. On October 4, 1967, the expiration date of the option which had then been twice postponed, Pan Am relieved the suspense. Mr. Trippe entered these discussions through a telephone call to Mr. Allen and agreement was finally reached that Boeing would participate in Pan Am's probable effort, a few years later, to sell nineteen of their earliest 707s which were not equipped with the newer JT3-D fan-jet engines. A new contract for the purchase of nineteen airplanes under terms similar to previous orders was then signed. The 747 negotiations again proceeded without reference to or possible interruption by the 707 purchase.

Parametric Studies. The Trippe proposal in mid-August for the early production of a greatly improved 747B had generated a series of parametric studies by the Boeing engineers in which varying airplane performances were calculated for engines of varying sizes, wing spans of varying widths, and proportionately varying gross weights. The Boeing engineers proposed to set forth such a series of studies so that the resulting tradeoffs could be compared and the most promising combination could then be selected for the 747Bs. To complete this series, the Boeing staff stated that five months would be required. The impatient Mr. Trippe called for a "status report" in one month. On September 28th Mr. Pennell and his engineering staff presented the analytical results of three stages of wing extension. Mr. Pennell concluded that, even without windtunnel tests, his studies had not met the Trippe requirements. Mr. Pennell observed in conclusion that it appeared that his next step was "back to the old drawing board." Mr. Trippe did not propose to ease the problem by softening his requirements for airplane performance.

On October 9th Mr. Trippe returned from London where he had conducted some conferences for the Intercontinental Hotel Corporation (wholly owned by Pan Am) and plunged back into the 747B project through several telephone conversations with Mr. Allen. Mr. Trippe was considering the procedure of using another "Letter of Intent" to cover the 747B which would include provision for the return of the original 747s to Boeing in exchange as the 747B aircraft became available.

Ten days later Mr. Trippe and Mr. Allen met in Washington during a White House session of the Business Advisory Council, of which each was a member. Mr. Trippe brought back Mr. Allen's concept of a suitable "Letter of Intent." His concept set forth Boeing's clear intent to produce an "advanced 747" with improved characteristics in late '72 or early '73. This intent obviously fell far short of the spectacular characteristics which Mr. Trippe was stating as a requirement for the fall of '71. The Allen letter contained no reference to the turn-in of Pan Am's initial 747s and nothing in the nature of delivery priorities. Its real purpose was set forth not too subtly in its concluding sentence ". . . it would be in the best interests of all concerned for your people and ours, to promptly sit down and agree on specification revisions for the twenty-five airplanes which you have purchased, around the 710,000 pound airplane as we have proposed."

Concern by Wall Street and the Press. The frequency of staff trips between Seattle and New York, the length of major conferences, and the absence of normal public announcements of progress and the involvement of the senior principals naturally led to speculation in informed aviation circles and in the press. In the month of October 1967, at least three news agencies and two financial advisory offices called different elements of Pan Am to discuss rumors that Pan Am was about to cancel its 747 contract, that Pan Am was unable to finance its 747 purchase, and other disturbing ideas.

In mid-October the senior aerospace writer for the Wall Street Journal, Mr. Richard C. Cooke, called General Kuter and stated that his sources said that Pan Am was holding its 747 contract in abeyance and pressing for a 747B for delivery on a date far earlier than either Boeing or Pratt and Whitney could countenance. He implied that the steadily lowering price of both Boeing and Pan Am common stock was related to those rumors.

Without delay General Kuter invited Mr. Cooke to join him and Vice-President Willis Player, Pan Am Public Relations and gave to Mr. Cooke a background account of the Pan Am - Boeing relationship. Examples were cited of the Pan Am - Boeing relationship ten years earlier when the 707 was taking shape. Emphasis was placed on Pan Am's progress in making preparations for the introduction of the 747 in accordance with the scheduled deliveries in the current contract. Pan Am's continuing series of prepayments in accord with the contract were pointed out, including the $29,205,875 payment just delivered. The Pan Am - Boeing staff discussions were outlined as the normal, natural, and healthy procedure of developing, producing, and operating new and advanced aircraft. Mr. Cooke had great influence with the informed financial and aviation writers. Thereafter there was a marked reduction in the volume and intensity of rumors of Pan Am - Boeing strife.

As a follow-up to Mr. Allen's "Letter of Intent," Mr. Spalding, Mr. Munson, and several legal and contract experts came from Seattle to the Pan Am Building with a brief case full of letters for discussion during the week of October 23rd. Included were three draft letters containing major changes in the contract and two master specification changes. After analysis of these five detailed cross-referenced papers, it became clear to Pan Am that their acceptance would in effect degrade the guarantees in all phases of airplane performance in Purchase Order 189 and also increase the costs to Pan Am. The papers appeared to Pan Am to be a legal and contractual maze which would resolve the problem in Boeing's favor very much as it stood in the Ten Foot TWX and its subsequent modifications. Mr. Blackwell, who handled these discussions, told Messrs. Spalding and Munson that he couldn't take those papers even for further consideration at staff level until they clearly stated that Pan Am would get what Pan Am ordered or Boeing would pay for the deficiencies. After many long telephone conversations with their superiors back in Seattle, this Boeing team picked up their papers and went home to try again. Meanwhile the parametric studies continued.

A little more progress was made in the Pratt & Whitney - Pan Am negotiations, which were proceeding concurrently with the major Boeing discussions. Pan Am had ordered forty-three JT9D-1 engines to serve as spares along with Pan Am's basic order for twenty-five 747 airplanes. Because the JT9D-1 had been superseded by the JT9D-3, that order had to be renegotiated. Since the JT9D-3 was a more powerful engine and somewhat heavier, Pratt & Whitney said that it had to cost more to build and its sale price must accordingly advance. Pan Am argued that the price agreed upon was for a suitable 747 engine and the responsibility for requiring the JT9D-3 rather than the JT9D-1 was a matter for Boeing and Pratt & Whitney to settle. Eventually a mutually equitable agreement was reached wherein Pratt & Whitney would participate with Pan Am in the future retro-fittings and modifications of the JT9D-3 as it went through its programmed increases in power.

In mid-October Messrs. Trippe and Allen were again scheduled to meet on matters other than the 747. This time they were scheduled to be head table guests at a political dinner in Seattle for Senator Warren G. Magnusson. In preparation for that meeting Mr. Trippe asked General Kuter to draw up for him a position paper with proposals for future action. An example of the prevailing staff cooperation which previously had been unusual in Pan Am was brought forth by Mr. Trippe's request. General Kuter was scheduled to meet with Mr. Jackson McGowan, President of the Douglas Division of MacDonald Douglas, in Santa Monica, California to discuss Douglas' new interest in a large, wide bodied trijet (later the DC-10) and other matters. Because Pan Am's interest in an airplane that might compete with the 747 should have a salutory effect on the Boeing staff, it was decided not to defer General Kuter's visit to Douglas. After further conversations, the position paper was prepared for Mr. Trippe by Mr. Harold E. Gray, the President of Pan Am, but for signature by General Kuter, the Vice-President - Technical Staff.

This position paper recited the areas of airplane performance in which the 747 with the JT9D-3 engines would remain subspecification until an engine like a JT9D-7 was available. The paper proposed that Pan Am should accept the subspecification aircraft provided that Boeing should bear at least half the cost of eventual conversion to a JT9D-7 including all engine and associated airframe modification costs. This position paper dealt in some detail with the two freighters (747F) which had been scheduled to be the last two airplanes to be delivered to Pan Am by Boeing. Because reductions in payload and range were more severe in the case of the 747F than in the straight passenger model 747, Boeing had elected to ignore the 747F until plans on the passenger model 747 were firm. In this position paper Pan Am proposed that the two 747Fs on order, with JT9D-3 engines, should be accepted only if Boeing agreed to produce five or six high performance freighters in the fall of '71 (as sister ships to the Trippe definition of a 747B) and take the two 747Fs back in trade at depreciated book value.

On Sunday morning October 19th, Mr. Trippe in Seattle called General Kuter in New York to outline the four-hour session he had with Mr. Allen and his top staff on October 17th. As was always the case, the exact use to which he had put the position paper was not disclosed. He had, however, been highly critical of the JT9D-3 powered 747 in both passenger and freighter configuration and implied that he might refuse to accept them without a guarantee that Boeing would bear the expense of bringing them up to specification as quickly as adequate power was available from Pratt & Whitney or any other engine manufacturer. (Douglas was discussing a new big engine with General Electric to power its big tri-jet and Lockheed was doing likewise with Rolls-Royce.)

He did relieve some of the pressure he had placed on producing a 747B by late '71 by suggesting that Mr. Wells and the Boeing engineers redirect their current effort to redesign a newer bigger wing to a "simple" extension of the current wing. In effect this change of interest redirected Boeing's efforts from parametric studies of future airplanes to possible modification of the current 747. Mr. Wells and the same staff of engineers had extended the 707 wing and effectively converted the initial 707 to a much improved and highly successful 707-321B. But, as always, the conference concluded with requirement for more power from an engine with the same geometry as the JT9D-3—something like a JT9D-7 with at least 47,500 pounds thrust at the outset. He also relaxed his requirement for an initial cruise altitude of 37,000 feet. His relaxation was not exactly revolutionary. He reduced that requirement to 36,000 feet. And finally Mr. Trippe directed General Kuter and the staff again to go to Hartford to stir up the fire under Pratt & Whitney to get them to produce at least 47,500 pounds thrust from their JT9D-3 engine shell at least two years earlier than they believed possible.

Once more the telephones between the Pan Am Building and the Pratt & Whitney plant became very active. Mr. Gwinn again agreed to study the methods of quickly producing 47,500 pounds of thrust from an engine with about the same dimensions as the JT9D-3. On November 24th he brought to New York with him Mr. Art Smith, then President of Pratt & Whitney (Mr. Gwinn having taken over the Chief Executive's post upon Mr. Horner's retirement), Mr. Barney

Schmickrath, an expert engineer recently appointed Executive Vice-President, Pratt & Whitney, plus members of the engineering staff. They had a long conference with the Pan Am engineers who were competent to discuss the technicalities of new high powered jet turbines: Vice-President Kauffman, Chief Engineer Borger, Engineer Walter Fry, and their staff. Again it was concluded that Pratt & Whitney had the knowledge and the technical skill to produce a higher powered engine in less time than Boeing could modify and produce a modified wing and airframe, if economics were no factor. Since the cost of a more powerful engine would be reflected in Boeing's price for the airplane and engines, the economics of a new engine was properly a matter of Pratt & Whitney/Boeing cognizance; cost was not discussed in any detail with Pan Am.

Pratt & Whitney then discussed their latest study with Boeing and a Boeing presentation or status report was made by Mr. Carl Munson and Boeing Engineer Olesen in the Pan Am Building on the 27th of November. Present on the Pan Am side were the negotiating team plus the President, Mr. Harold E. Gray and the member of the Board of Directors who had from the beginning been the outside Board Member with the closest interest and most complete knowledge of the 747—General Charles A. Lindbergh. At this meeting the Boeing engineers concluded that even a minor extension of the wing tips or an extension of the wing roots would require new wing jigs and new engine mounts and positions to assure against a dangerous flutter in the already highly engineered wing. A "minor" wing extension was consequently judged to be impossible. It was concluded that a 747 which would meet all specifications and otherwise meet the conditions which Mr. Trippe, Mr. Gray, and the staff had defined as "acceptable" would require a delay in production till late 1972 or even early 1973.

New Objective. General Kuter reviewed this situation with Mr. Trippe, with General Lindbergh present. Mr. Trippe had never believed that anything was impossible. In this case however he could not debate the economics of developments which were completely outside Pan Am's ken or control—the costs of more power and the costs and delays related to the redesign of wings and airframes. The conclusion was to continue all efforts to force Boeing and Pratt & Whitney to produce on schedule a 747 approaching as closely as possible the performances set forth in the specification and then to get from Boeing the best deal possible in the future process of improving performance by retrofit and modification or by turn-in and replacement by an eventual 747B. While this was not a substantial change in corporate policy, this conference did clarify and sharpen up Pan Am's objectives in the continuing discussions with Boeing.

Four months had passed since the last official statement from Pan Am in which Mr. Gray specifically stated that the modification of the contract proposed in the Ten Foot TWX on August 3rd was unacceptable. Mr. Boullioun telephoned General Kuter to state that hardware was collecting from many subcontractors, the first few 747s were beginning to take form in the Everett plant, Mr. Trippe and Mr. Allen were having intermittent private conversations whose results were frequently interpreted quite differently in Seattle and in the Pan Am Building, negotiators at several levels were meeting and reporting results of conferences, and "wheel-spinning and misunderstandings were almost inevitable."

Tripartite Review. As a result of Mr. Boullioun's call, he with Messrs. Pennell and Munson, Mr. Art Smith with Mr.

Barney Schmickrath from Pratt & Whitney, and General Kuter with Mr. Borger met on December 19th in the Hotel Pierre in New York for a room-service dinner conference which lasted until well after midnight. From this conference one sizeable step forward was made in Mr. Smith's personal assurance that Pratt & Whitney would make more power available in the JT9D-3 engine by providing water-injection by the end of 1969. By injecting distilled water into the combustion chambers during full power take-off, the JT9D-3 would attain 45,000 pounds of thrust for the moments required to take-off. This added thrust on short flights would permit substantial increases in payload. On longer flights more fuel could be carried resulting in substantial increases in range. Mr. Smith estimated that this improvement would be made for $15,000 per engine. $15,000 for each of four engines (and the spares) was not considered inconsequential, but on an $800,000 engine, $15,000 represented only about a two percent increase in cost for a very important increase in power. With that power increase, Mr. Boullioun believed that he could define an acceptable 747F in about one more month. Both Mr. Smith and Mr. Boullioun were personally and officially solid in their views that all economic considerations proved that there could not be an advanced airplane "like the 747B" with a 50,000 pound or so JT9D-7 earlier than 1972. Pan Am recognized that there were economic limits to these great manufacturers' capabilities but still believed that Pratt & Whitney had the talent to produce more power and Boeing had the skill to further reduce airframe weight without sacrifice of strength. It was a long evening during which respected personal and corporate friends were all pressing for optimum safe airplane performance without jeopardy to a reasonable margin of profit for their companies.

The next Pan Am - Boeing discussion occurred in Los

Angeles under somewhat unusual and cosmopolitan circumstances. Upon the request from the Military Airlift Command of the United States Air Force, the National Defense Transportation Association had organized an advisory committee of representative civilian experts. One of the five panels of the NDTA/MAC committee was the Operations Panel of which General Kuter (Pan Am) was chairman and the panel members included Mr. Boullioun (Boeing), Mr. Jackson R. McGowan (Douglas), Mr. Haughton (Lockheed), and several airline executives. On January 12-13, 1968 the NDTA/MAC committee met at the Douglas plant where the Military Airlift Command's new Air Evacuation DC-9 was being delivered and, incidentally, where an elaborate briefing was delivered and inspection made of the Douglas Aircraft Division's new big tri-jet DC-10, a major competitor to Boeing's 747 and a direct competitor to Lockheed's tri-jet L-1011. After this "cosmopolitan" conference, General Kuter and Mr. Boullioun met privately for a review of the status of their 747 problems.

Mr. Boullioun's review concluded with Mr. Allen's offer to come to New York to present to Mr. Trippe the conclusions of their study of a "modest" wing improvement and the early provision of more engine power. Since the overall conclusions would be in line with the results of the triangular dinner conference in Hotel Pierre a month earlier, General Kuter said that such conclusions would not make a trip by Mr. Allen worthwhile as they did not provide any new basis for corporate agreement. As a new point of discussion, General Kuter suggested cancelling the 747F altogether and reviving the freighter version after a truly advanced 747 was produced, perhaps not until 1973. Since the currently proposed freighter came far from offering the economics that even the short route operators had expected, Mr. Boullioun recognized the advantages of cancelling the freighter but feared that the contracts with one or more of Boeing's lesser customers might force the company to produce one or two freighters. The cost of "hand-making" a very few such airplanes would give to Boeing a new and very expensive problem to add to their already overlong list.

Meanwhile a considerable number of contract changes and revisions of agreement were processed and executed through normal staff interplay. The controversial items, those related to reductions in performance specifications without compensating reductions in price, were held in abeyance.

On February 2, 1968 Mr. Allen addressed a letter to Mr. Trippe which put into the written record many of the Boullioun-Kuter conversations in December and January. He suggested a conference on April 15th to firm-up the proposal to get added thrust for take-off by adding water-injection and a new plan to increase the authorized maximum gross weight to 730,000 pounds which, with added take-off power, would increase the payload-range capabilities of the 747. By April 15th he would have data on the extent of increases in noise and decreases in cruise altitude and speed which would result from this weight.

Ten days later a long scheduled meeting of Pan Am's Board of Directors was held in Seattle where the Board could visit the mock-up of the 747 interior. This was the first opportunity the outside directors had been given to see the developing airplane. Many comments and observations were made concerning the probable passenger appeal of the interior decoration of the wide-bodied transport. While they had been told and had seen sketches of interiors that were rooms rather than tubes, and a spiral stairway that led to a gracious cocktail lounge, they felt that it had to be seen to be believed and they were confident of enthusiastic passenger acceptance. There were no discussions of the status of the 747 contract when the Board was in Seattle.

On 1 March another $29,609,000 advance payment was transmitted by a Kuter-Connelly letter which again stated that Pan Am was living up to every element of its side of the contract and implied that Boeing was expected to do likewise.

On 7 March a Boeing letter was dispatched, in routine customer-relations form, presumably to all airlines that had ordered 747s. The letter described the availability of water-injection and increased authorized take-off weight as outlined in the Allen-Trippe letter of 2 February. The conference Mr. Allen had proposed in that letter was set up for the period March 11-15 when Mr. and Mrs. Allen were scheduled to visit in the Trippe's house on the golf course of the Cotton Bay Club on Eleuthera Island in the Bahamas.

To prepare for the Eleuthera Meeting, a series of staff briefings were held with Mr. Trippe and Mr. Gray, who participated in most of them. While it had not been announced, Mr. Trippe was planning to retire and had consequently brought Mr. Gray more directly into the Pan Am - Boeing negotiations. Mr. Trippe and Mr. Gray carried with them to Eleuthera the substance of these briefings in the form of a draft letter from Pan Am to Boeing, which was intended to identify all controversial points in the 747 negotiations and propose a resolution for each.

The letter identified each of the shortcomings in the current concept of the 747 and itemized the financial impact on the earning power of each. The letter proposed that Boeing reimburse Pan Am for each until the shortcoming was remedied. As examples, it was concluded that Pan Am would have to pay an additional $49,000 per airplane per year solely for the fuel required to carry the anticipated 15,010 pound airframe overweight; $25,000 per airplane per year for the added engine maintenance cost related to the requirement to change from the JT9D-1 to the more powerful JT9D-3 engines;

$100,000 per airplane per year for added delays and added flying time caused by inability to fly above the existing trans-Atlantic traffic, and many more items of expense equally difficult to compute with precision. All such items extended over a fifteen year period were computed as adding three million dollars per airplane to the direct operating cost as a result of Boeing's failure to meet all performance guarantees. While no one in Pan Am expected Boeing to accept all or perhaps any of such computations, it was expected that they would point up the gravity with which Pan Am viewed those shortcomings. The letter described the 747Fs as completely unacceptable and proposed that they be deferred until an advanced 747B was offered, Boeing meanwhile to return the nine million dollars already advanced on the 747Fs plus interest at the prime rate.

Upon Mr. Trippe's and Mr. Gray's return from Eleuthera, the staff was informed that each of the items in the draft letter had been brought into the conversations which were held from time to time with Mr. Allen but no agreements or definite conclusions were reached on any of them.

Following the top level meeting at Eleuthera were the usual series of telephone calls between Seattle and New York as the staffs attempted to reconcile their versions of what their chiefs had proposed, rejected, or agreed. It was concluded that the contentious points had been enumerated but no appreciable progress had been made toward solutions for any.

Staff discussions for the next two months were summarized on May 7, 1968 by another Connelly-Kuter letter in which Boeing presented their version of contentious points in a series of proposed changes in the 747 contract. In the draft revision of the Purchase Agreement 189 which was numbered 189-15, Boeing set forth a series of new nominal performance guarantees which did not degrade the original nominal guarantees quite so severely as they had proposed previously. Each of these nominal guarantees included a plus or minus margin. For example, a guaranteed manufacturers weight empty of 296,400 pounds included a tolerance of two and one half percent which, in effect guaranteed that the weight would be not more than 303,810 pounds or less than 288,990 pounds. Pan Am's practical approach as well as past experience led to the consideration of every guarantee as the nominal modified by the most adverse tolerance. When all adverse tolerances were applied, the new guarantees still fell short of what Pan Am believed acceptable. In this May 7th letter Pan Am cited as a step in the right direction the absence of the previous demands that Pan Am would have to increase their contractual payments to cover the remedial changes. In the May 7th letter Boeing was specific in stating that Boeing would pay the added costs of converting from the JT9D-1 engine to the JT9D-3 and also for most of the added expense of providing water-injection equipment for the JT9D-3.

The letter urged that the staffs should meet as quickly as the contents of the letter could be studied with a view toward early agreement. Agreement with this letter in full would have resolved all contentious points and resulted in a contract modified in degrees acceptable to Boeing. Pan Am responded by telephone early on May 9th when General Kuter told Mr. Connelly that the staffs might meet without delay, that Pan Am noted the absence of previous requirements for Pan Am to make added payments for airplane and engine changes required, but also that the degree of degradation of original performance guarantees was still not acceptable to Pan Am.

The significant guarantees of performance set forth in this letter included:

MODIFIED SPECIFICATIONS	CONTRACT SPECIFICATIONS
Speed: Mach .89 plus or minus 2% 541 knots plus or minus 2%	.877
Take-off: 11,750 feet plus or minus 750 feet	9,900
Approach Speed: 135 knots maximum	
Initial Cruise Altitude: 31,600 feet plus or 1,500 feet at speed of 0.84M	33,000 minimum
Take-off Noise: 115 PNdb plus or minus 3 PNdb	113-117
Approach Noise: 109 PNdb plus or minus 3 PNdb	

On 31 May the now routine Kuter-Connelly letter transmitted another $29,609,000 prepayment from Pan Am to Boeing, again pointing out that Pan Am was living up to its side of the contract.

Change in Pan Am Line Up. Mr. Trippe had stepped down and appointed Mr. Gray to be the new, and only the second, Chief Executive, Pan American World Airways. Concurrently General Kuter telephoned Mr. Boullioun. General Kuter described Mr. Gray as a practical realist, a former pioneer instrument pilot, and a precisionist in all matters. Along with all members of the staff, Mr. Gray was puzzled by Pan Am's continuing to pay over $29,000,000 every quarter for twenty-three passenger airplanes which would not meet specifications and two freighters which Boeing probably would not build or which would be so far below specification that Pan Am wouldn't think of accepting. The Pan Am Treasurer was not "puzzled" by the payments, he was furious. As the new Chief Executive, Mr. Gray recognized that the 747 contract was a "mess" and no credit to either Boeing or Pan Am. His last direct participation in the matter had been his telephone call to Mr. Yeasting in August, ten months previous, when he made it clear that full payment by Pan Am for aircraft which could not live up to their guaranteed performance was out of the question. During those ten months he had received no word other than reports from inconclusive meetings. General Kuter said that it seemed clear that a resolution of the contract "mess" depended on the length Boeing would go to compensate Pan Am for the anticipatory breaches of the current contract.

Continuing this lengthy telephone conversation, again summarizing the basic issues in contention, General Kuter recognized the great efforts by the Boeing staff to prove that the 747 with the JT9D-3 engine and water-injection would carry bigger payloads which, on Pan Am routes, should increase earnings by $40,000 per airplane per year after it was authorized to take-off at 710,000 pounds gross weight. He observed that added earnings approaching another $40,000 were possible after the FAA had certificated the 710,000 pound TOGW, but that certification was not scheduled till the fall of the first year of 747 operation and maximum loads were rarely attained in the fall, winter, and spring. Of much more importance, he insisted that the Boeing staff ignored the added cost of operating the heavier airplane with water-injection, which the Pan Am staff estimated would be $100,000 per airplane per year.

Mr. Boullioun, after a pause, said that he was recording the conversation and asked, "Do you have anything further?" General Kuter's response was, "Isn't that enough?"

It was agreed that a freighter which would be acceptable to Pan Am was unlikely to be produced for delivery until 1973 and that the Boeing and Pan Am staffs had been working from the same basic data but had been coming up with conclusions that could not be reconciled. Largely on Mr. Boullioun's recommendation, it was also agreed that the time had come to get the principals of both corporations alone and without their staffs to sit down and decide how to proceed. It was agreed to try to arrange a meeting in mid-June between Messrs. Allen, Wilson, and Boullioun on the Boeing side and Gray, Kuter, and an officer new to this negotiation problem, Mr. Najeeb E. Halaby, newly elected President, Pan American World Airways.

New Blood. Mr. Halaby had joined Pan Am in 1965 as the 747 project was taking form. Because his initial assignment as a Senior Vice-President was centered around Pan Am's Business Jet and other diversification interests and also because Mr. Trippe chose to handle the 747 projects with a small staff, Mr. Halaby had not been in the main stream of the 747 development. On the other hand, because of his background as a test pilot in the U.S. Navy, a lawyer, a Los Angeles aerospace businessman, and then as the Administrator of the Federal Aviation Administration, Mr. Halaby was highly qualified to enter and to handle the program. Recognizing Mr. Halaby's unique qualification and his logical interest, General Kuter had brought him up to date from time to time and had received his views and opinions concerning the 747 negotiations. While his presence was new to these negotiation teams, corporate negotiation was nothing new to Mr. Halaby and he was well versed in the 747 program.

Again the staff worked up position papers in preparation for this top-level conference. Plan No. 1, "Big Stick," to accept the first fifteen sub-specification 747s and cancel the last ten was compared with Plan No. 2, "Olive Branch," to accept twenty-five and options for fifteen 747Bs in '72 and twenty 747Bs in '73 (with provisions for the return of the initial twenty-five) and with Plan No. 3, "Stand Pat," to continue to insist that the cost to Pan Am of a sub-specification airplane would be proportionately below contract cost. It was generally decided to enter with Plan No. 3 and if Boeing proposed concessions, to adjust toward Plan No. 2.

A conference was held in the Sky Club atop the Pan Am Building between Messrs. Allen, Wilson, and Boullioun and Messrs. Gray, Halaby, and Kuter from noon till five PM in a private dining room on the 13th of June. Although the Boeing officers may have felt that they had been dealing previously with the individual views of Mr. Juan T. Trippe, after that five-hour session it must have been clear that the solid Pan Am corporate view was every bit as firm on the part of the new Chairman and Chief Executive, the new President, and the newly elected Executive Vice-President— General Kuter also having been promoted when Mr. Trippe stepped down.

It was no surprise to the newly promoted Pan Am officers that they won no concessions from the Boeing officers at that first engagement. There was agreement that the Boeing staff would make some further studies and report back once again to the Pan Am staff.

During July and August some impetus was added by the public interest in the roll-out ceremonies for the first 747 which had been scheduled for September 30, 1968. As the pace picked up at the Everett factory, it became more urgent that there be a Pan Am - Boeing agreement before the publicity peak scheduled for the last day of September. The impetus of another twenty-nine million dollar prepayment due on 1 September was also felt by both parties.

Progress was made toward solving the freighter problem. Boeing conceded that the performance of the two 747Fs in the contract at the time of their scheduled delivery, one in July and one in August of 1970, would fall far short of what either Boeing or Pan Am considered acceptable and proposed that passenger models be substituted for these two much heavier and more complicated freight carriers. A year or so later, with JT9D-3 wet engines and an authorized weight of 730,000 or 733,000 pounds, the 747F would be much more attractive. Concurrently American, National, and United Airlines had entered discussions with Pan Am concerning the lease of early 747 passenger models. Pan Am quickly concluded that it would be highly advantageous to receive the high rental rates that two early 747s could command and agreed to accept the passenger rather than the freighter models as the last two of the original order for twenty-five 747s.

With the 747F problem solved, the major remaining point of contention was centered around the JT9D-3W ("W" for "wet" or water-injection) power plant. The JT9D-3W was required because the original engine did not generate enough take-off thrust to provide acceptable payload-range characteristics for the 747. Yet the JT9D-3W was heavier, more expensive, and more costly to operate and maintain. Again Pan Am maintained that Boeing should pay the added costs because the added power was needed to meet or approach contractual specifications that could not otherwise be met as a result of the overweight Boeing had built into the airframe. These installation costs were computed to cost either Pan Am or Boeing almost $5,000,000 and the added operating expenses were estimated to be some $113,000 per airplane per year. Here again was a version of the continuing problem—whose fault, how much would it cost, and who should pay?

Less than a week before the roll-out ceremonies, in a letter dated September 24, 1968, Boeing proposed a compromise on costs and a modification in methods of compensation for added expense. Agreement was eventually reached on a series of arrangements which included new and improved performance guarantees for the fall of '71 when the larger JT9D-7 would be available. Included also were some improvements in Boeing's warranty on the airframe and a curtailment on previously established rates of escalation for payments on the airplane. Boeing also agreed to credit Pan Am with approximately half of the added cost associated with the requirement for water-injection on the JT9D-3. Consequently Pan Am and Boeing could appear jointly at the widely publicized roll-out of 747 Number ONE as the proud parents of the airplane and advise the trade press that the negotiations attending the developing airplane design and construction had been concluded with mutual satisfaction.

Chapter 3

The Struggle for Delivery on Schedule

September 1968–December 1969

While Chiefs Argued, Workers Built Airplanes. In early 1966 after contracts were signed and the final decision was made to proceed with the 747 program, Boeing moved vigorously into all the physical aspects of the program. Evidence was seen first at Everett, Washington, in the clearing of the alder and fir forest alongside the once busy USAF Paine Field to make way for one of the largest buildings in the world, the new 747 factory. Various airplane parts began to take shape in Boeing's other plants and in the factories of scores of subcontractors. These parts were designed to fit together and their manufacture was timed to arrive at the Everett plant as soon as the plant could be completed to accept them and as soon as the special trains and rail lines could be produced to transport the parts.

Pan Am's initial association with 747 hardware was minor and scattered but became more and more direct as the first airframes began to take shape and as the test engines were assembled. All during the year and a half of study, conference, confrontation, adjustment, and final settlement of overweight and under-performance problems, negotiators on both sides of the tables found pleasant relief from the analytical and

September 1968–December 1969

theoretical computations that generated seemingly unending controversy by escaping from offices and conference rooms and visiting the aircraft plants in Seattle and the engine plant in Hartford. The incubating airframes and engines and decisions on many related components of hardware, furniture, fixtures, and the complicated and elaborate equipment offered happy escape to Pan Am's staff. The physical airplane and engine assemblies were far more interesting than the maze of words in the conference rooms and contracts.

In Seattle, Boeing had constructed a series of plywood replicas of 747 cabin interiors. In these mock-ups the several manufacturers and decorators exhibited their concepts and offerings to Boeing and to the airlines. Boeing also built mock-ups or replicas of the control cabin in which the several airline operational authorities could discuss and select types and locations of instruments and operational items. The control cabin had been laid out initially by the Boeing engineering flight crew that was scheduled to test fly the airplane. They worked in close collaboration with Captain Scott Flower, Pan Am's long time Chief Pilot-Technical, who was widely recognized by the other airlines as well as Boeing as the primary airline designer of the highly efficient cockpit in the 707 and 727. Captain Flower insisted upon the conventional circular cockpit instruments while the TWA pilots wanted the vertical digital type instruments favored by the Air Force and Lockheed. The eventual decision favored the circular or dial-type instruments with additional digital read-outs where practical.

Boeing also built a metal engineering mock-up of the main members of the airframe itself, in which Boeing and Pan Am technical staffs spent many hours discussing the new problems that would arise with the big new airplane. Facilities for quick emergency evacuation from high levels by large numbers of people was only one of the substantial new problems created by the huge scale and dimensions of the 747.

Pan Am also constructed some minor 747 interior mock-ups in which their own designers and decorators could create and decide on items that they wished, at least initially, to be exclusive with Pan Am. When concepts were laid out in the Boeing mock-ups, they immediately became known and could be copied or ordered directly by other airlines—the Pan Am conceived top-deck lounge and circular stairway to wit.

As the time of roll-out drew near, increasing numbers of decisions as to components and other matters were required. Since great pictorial coverage of the roll-out was assured and since Pan Am would receive operational 747s well before any other carrier, Pan Am maintained that 747 Number ONE should roll-out in the traditional blue and white Pan Am paint pattern, "Blue-Ball" on the tail and all. Boeing knew full well that Pan Am had bought and had already paid substantially for the first five, five of the next ten, five of the following ten, etc. up to twenty-three passenger 747s. Boeing knew equally well that their own economic future depended upon selling far greater numbers of airplanes to those airlines who were still waiting to see the final production airplane. Boeing elected therefore to paint 747 Number ONE in a Boeing paint pattern and to try to pacify Pan Am with the suggestion that first flights were not always successful and perhaps the "Blue Ball" should not be exposed to a possible public failure in the initial flight.

Roll Out. The last days of August were tense in Seattle and particularly in the Boeing 747 plant at Everett. Boeing's vice-president and plant manager, Mr. Malcolm T. Stamper, a respected intercollegiate athlete at Georgia Tech some twenty years earlier, had his production team keyed up for their big competition in the world of airplane manufacture.

September 1968–December 1969

For well over a year Boeing had announced that the 747 was on schedule. Complicated, newly designed or invented, subcontracted parts from major manufacturers all over the country were arriving more or less on schedule and were tested upon arrival and fitted together. When they lagged in time of arrival or were not produced to exact dimensions, Stamper's team was on the next airplane to assure that the subcontractor would perform. The PERT and other management charts that coordinated this record-making undertaking covered large walls in big rooms in the Everett factory. Mr. Stamper and staff had been living with these charts. Roll-out on 1 October 1968 as scheduled was the initial critical date which would tell the world whether or not Boeing really had full control.

The guests were arriving before the last titanium bolt was fitted and no one breathed easy until an unusually bright and warm sunlit morning dawned in Everett on that last day of September 1968.

Many distinguished guests, seated in a special pavillion, watched the enormous doors on one of the world's largest buildings slide open. Even the smooth operation of these enormous doors was an engineering problem of some magnitude. The fact that the doors would open on time and smoothly set the pattern for a successful day. Framed in the opening left by the sliding doors was 747 NUMBER ONE in glistening white paint. The airline devices of the twenty-six major airlines that had already ordered airplanes were placed below the name "Boeing 747.". While no larger than others, Pan Am could find some solace in the fact that the "Blue Ball" led all the rest.

As Mr. Trippe and Mr. Allen shook hands, 747 Number ONE was towed slowly and majestically to a special ramp that had been built at about second-story level above the parking apron. Twenty-six carefully selected stewardesses in the newest uniforms of their twenty-six major airlines were awaiting on that second-story level, each with her bottle of champagne to splash over her proper airline device in this unique paint pattern.

Even the designers and engineers who had worked on the 747 seemed surprised that it did not appear to be gross or bulky in defiance of the clumsy title "Jumbo" that the blasé press had hung on it. All knew that it was more than twice as heavy as any 707, more than twice as long as the Wright Brothers' first flight and had a tail that stood over six stories above the ground; nevertheless it looked more majestic than massive. The reason became slowly apparent when it was realized that the hangar door space alone was in about the same proportion as the standard hangar designed to accommodate a 707. The 100,000-pound tow truck for the 747 was about proportional to the normal tow for a 707, and the 747's dimensions were in graceful harmony with one another, as well as with the hangar doors and the tow tug. All in perspective, the results were most gratifying to the developers of the 747.

In the pavillion with distinguished guests, many visitors and representatives, and groups of Boeing workers, there were appropriate speeches, much congratulating and well wishing. After the formal presentations, many many pictures were taken of attractive stewardesses standing in the shrouds for the big fans in front of the big jet engines. The guests walked through the giant plane and were awed by the immensity of it and also by the vast space within the structure of the hangar.

After the formal ceremonies of the roll-out and while the visitors and spectators were walking around on the ramp outside the factory and admiring the shiny new potential breakthrough into the '70s, Mr. Stamper took General Kuter on a tour through the plant. Huge placards and billboard-size flow charts were there in evidence of the carefully programmed work that produced Number ONE not only on schedule but one day earlier. Number Two, Number Three, and on down the line were visible in their respective positions in the assembly process. General Kuter was impressed by the gathering of parts at the last identified point in the line, which was set up as 747 Number Eleven. He congratulated Mr. Stamper on the evidence of Boeing's confidence in the success of this Boeing - Pan Am businessman's risk. Beginning the assembly of the eleventh airplane before the first could prove that it would fly, or even taxi, evidenced confidence of the highest order.

Most of the guests were transported back to Seattle on the train over the special tracks built to haul the heavy materials up to the newly constructed plant for the 747 at Everett. 747 Number ONE was then promptly towed back into its hangar for the many weeks of remaining work to get it in condition for first critical flight, its subsequent testing and proving, and its all important certification by the FAA as safe and suitable for airline operation.

747 Flies! From roll-out on 30 September 1968 until 9 February 1969 with some delays due to labor union negotiations and some due to the exceedingly severe winter in Washington State, the Boeing and Pratt & Whitney production people had their hands full in getting 747 Number One through its ground and taxi testing and ready to fly. Finally, on 9 February, from Paine Field, the strip alongside the factory at Everett, Boeing's top test flight crew took off uneventfully before the vastly relieved presence of Messrs. Allen, Wilson, Boullioun, and thousands of Boeing workmen as well as the Pan Am representative and staff. The first lift-off, the first climb, the first simple maneuvers, and the first landing and stop went as the designer had intended. By the 27th of February, eight flights totaling twelve hours and twenty-eight minutes had been completed and 747 Number One was then flown from Paine Field in Everett to the much shorter old Boeing Field in Seattle for some two weeks of installation of flutter equipment and other test gear. The twelve hours and twenty-eight minutes of flying had produced enough flight data to justify the preliminary flight evaluation which was scheduled for that time period.

The results of the first eight flights were reassuring. Pan Am's chief test pilot, Captain Scott Flower, had been aboard early flights. The Pan Am staff and the Boeing staff worked over the initial flight evaluation and the report presented to the Pan Am Board of Directors by Mr. Halaby in March. The report included: successful performance under many conditions of stall which exceeded the established FAA safety and airworthiness requirements; airplane handling characteristics were at least as good as those on the highly successful 707; and noise levels were much lower than anticipated. Boeing and Pan Am also evaluated the initial performance of the Pratt & Whitney's JT9D test engines. Their conclusions were that the engines had been exceptionally trouble-free. It was significant that certain tests of engine exhaust patterns could not be made because the JT9D engine generated so little smoke that the exhaust pattern could not be seen. Engines had been shut down in flight and restarted without difficulty and the reverse thrust was sufficiently prompt and powerful to provide abundant braking for the heaviest 747.

Revised Detailed Flight Test Program. Boeing then published a revised flight test program which showed in detail the type testing that each of the five predesignated 747s would have to undergo to satisfy Boeing, Pan Am, the other airlines, as well as the FAA that the airplanes were safe and suitable for unlimited passenger service. A total of 1377 flying hours were programmed, 810 of which were to satisfy Boeing's and the airlines' own requirements and 567 of which were specifically set aside for the FAA's test and certification purposes. If for no other reason than the size of the airplane and its capability of carrying huge passenger loads, the FAA's requirements for the 747 certification process were more demanding than those that had ever been applied to any other airplane. The 747 and its engines were fresh off the drawing boards and other transports and engines had some military predecessors which had worked out most of the "bugs" that always appear in a new aircraft and new engines. Because the 747 was a spectacular new development, it would get world-wide attention, and many foreign governments would be very critical when it was about to enter their airspace or operate from their airdromes and compete for their passengers. By virtue of membership in the International Civil Aviation Organization, a specialized agency of the United Nations, all nations were bound to accept the FAA's certificate as evidence that the 747 was safe to carry passengers of all nations, safe to fly over foreign countries, and safe to operate on foreign airports. The FAA had no choice but to be demanding, and both the manufacturer and the airlines agreed that standards should be higher for the 747 than for preceding aircraft.

Extreme Precaution. These special considerations governing the FAA's tests produced some delays in the program that had not been anticipated. It was not anticipated that the FAA would at times have upwards of two hundred inspectors on 747 Number One. That number not only interfered with Boeing workmen but they interfered occasionally with each other. Also it was not anticipated that the FAA would make a practice of adding new and more demanding tests as the flying proceeded. Still, in view of the importance of all safety considerations, no actual complaints were registered because of these delays and extensions in the test program.

Five Test Airplanes. From the beginning, the first five 747s in the production line had been scheduled for the test flight and certification program. Number One was the property of Boeing and featured in the roll-out ceremony. Number One was scheduled primarily for the rigorous aerodynamic airframe tests during 388 hours of flying. Number Two was scheduled to roll-out in early January 1969, fly sixty days later, and be primarily involved in 330 hours of testing of major components including engines. This airplane would eventually be owned by Pan Am. After testing, it would return to the factory for rework and refurbishing and eventually emerge as Number forty-one in the production line. Number Three would require almost four months after roll-out to be equipped with a great array of interconnected drums of water and pumps to fill drums and to move the water loading from fore to aft or side to side in order to flight test with all varieties of cargo and passenger loadings. Number Three was also scheduled for tests of the airplane's elaborate hydraulic and pneumatic systems, smoke detection systems, and fire extinguishing systems. It was planned for 147 hours of test flying. It was also a Pan Am airplane, eventually to be the thirty-sixth through the production line. Number Four, also a Pan Am machine, was the most interesting to the public and to all those involved in passenger service. It was the test item which was to prove the 747's suitability for passenger accommodation to include acoustics, oxygen systems, emergency evacuation, and all aspects of passenger comfort and safety. It was the only test airplane to have its interior completed and it was therefore the most photographed of the lot and also the test airplane in which the FAA would authorize airline officials, aviation press, and like passengers to ride from time to time when testing was not critical. After 312 hours of test flying it would return to the factory to emerge as the thirty-second airplane through final production and the eighteenth to be delivered to Pan Am. The contract called for its delivery in April 1970. Number Five was scheduled for eventual delivery to TWA after two hundred hours of testing performance at low speeds, icing and anti-icing, and certain stall characteristics. The interlocking long-term aspects of the aircraft for the flight test program were typical of the vast and detailed programing problems constantly faced by Boeing's production staff.

As a whole, the flight test and the certification programs moved with exceptional smoothness particularly in view of the many new and untried elements of airframe, engines, and the whole array of newer and bigger accessories required by this huge and advanced airplane. The program had its rough moments; each of them appeared at critical times and each became its own cliff-hanging crisis.

Incidents of varying dimensions delayed the flight test program from the beginning. Severe weather after roll-out delayed the first flight. Some technical problems were related to that extraordinary winter in Washington State. One unexpected delay was traced to the great thrust of the big fan-jet engines. It was discovered that it was not feasible even to run up those engines if there was the least bit of ice or snow on the airport pavement. Ordinary chocks on salted pavement were of no avail against the vast power of the JT9Ds.

Even more difficulties were related to press coverage than to aerodynamic problems or technical matters. With each crisis, the "death watch" attitude of the press became more and more apparent. Ambitious young writers were discovering that their editors would give them by-lines for "disclosing, revealing, or uncovering" negative or unfavorable items. Forecast 747 accidents won headlines of "genocide." Forecast smoke or noise from the new, powerful, but untested JT9D-3 engines were played up by the new school of popular but novice ecologists. Finally the apocalyptic press set up, in effect, a death watch on the 747 which magnified the negative factors and ignored the accomplishments. Unhappily some of the doomsday writers were fed speculative adverse material by airlines or governments which had missed out on early delivery positions for 747s. As the U.S. press would publish alarms, the foreign press would pick them up and embellish them. Then foreign aviation authorities would call for more stringent criteria. The FAA, which was under a politically appointed Administrator, would usually respond to all by adding new test requirements and extending the time required to test.

Another example of such sequence was the furor over the 747 'wake'. In taxiing the 747 in Seattle, an improperly parked light airplane and an employee's Volkswagen had been rolled over. A small jet aircraft, while trying to photograph the 747 in flight, had maneuvered into its wing-wash and jet-exhaust and it had been upset. The press had headlined these incidents as catastrophic phenomena peculiar to the high-powered "jumbo" with no reference to improper parking or normal jet wake. Eventually in February from France, Italy, and to some extent from London came observations that this new giant American airplane about to be introduced by American free-enterprise airlines should not be permitted in their skies if it generated disasters by its wake. As a result the FAA temporarily insisted that traffic controllers keep all other aircraft two thousand feet above or below and no closer than five miles behind the 747 pending the completion of new tests. Smoke generators then had to be installed in a test 747 and it was required to fly many hours over test ranges in an elaborate series of new, expensive, and time consuming tests

September 1968–December 1969

to prove what had been known by Boeing engineers and flight test crews from the outset. Smaller and slower aircraft always encounter severe turbulence when flown too close behind bigger faster ones. This conclusion had been known by boat pilots before the days of Columbus. The wake of the 747 was eventually proved to be little if any more vigorous than the wake of the 707 or DC8 and certainly far less than the French-English Concorde or the USAF B-71. The critical press accepted the conclusion but accepted it slowly and then focused its attention on other problems.

"Ovalizing" of the JT9D engines became a publicized problem and it was headlined as "engine failure" with implications that it was not safe to fly. Ovalizing was a difficulty which developed after many hundreds of hours of flying. The cause and the remedy were soon found. Fan-jet engines are essentially cylindrical tubes against which a powerful fan pulls at the fore-end and a jet blast pushes at the aft-end. The big JT9D-3 fan-jet was hung under the wings by two lugs, one fore and one aft, while smaller engines had previously been suspended by a single lug in the mid-section of the cylindrical tube. During the test flying, it was discovered that the hot very high speed rotors inside the cylinders were wearing the circular cross section of the stators in the cylinder into an oval shape, with some resultant loss of power and greatly increased rate of fuel consumption. This "ovalizing" was deduced to be the result of bending of the engine case tube because the great pull of the forward fan generated torque which bent the tube downward between the fore and aft lugs. To fix this "bug", a steel "Y" shaped yoke was designed to stiffen the tube to stop the bending between the two points of suspension.

After many weeks, the FAA and the press concluded that "ovalizing" would continue until engines with the Y-yoke stiffener could be installed, but the penalty for ovalizing was not safety or reliability but economic as a result of getting less power while consuming more jet fuel. Later on in the development experience, there were a couple of engine fires caused by manifold cracking and a series of failures in small, improperly heat-treated pins that attached blades to hubs in the jet engine rotors. Again, the blade failures were treated by the press as much greater hazards to safety than the facts warranted; and then the press speculated that the FAA might or should ground all 747s until a fix was completed. In every case, however, there was abundant power available in three or even in two remaining engines to permit the completion of all flights with no prejudice to safety. Until these pins were replaced there was a penalty to regularity and reliability, but no penalty to safety. A great increase in the frequency and extent of inspection of engines between flights was called for, and then the FAA slowly convinced the foreign and domestic press that safety had never been prejudiced.

The test program provided a basis for periods of close cooperation and some periods of sharp controversy between the Boeing and the Pan Am staffs. In the cases of FAA and press criticism and demand, Pan Am's proximity and Boeing's isolation from centers of authority in New York and Washington resulted in the Pan Am staff acting and speaking for Boeing on some matters requiring quick, on-the-spot, topside discussions.

One period of sharp Pan Am - Boeing controversy was generated by T. Wilson's last minute decision to fly test 747 Number Four from Seattle to Paris for the airshow at Le Bourget Airport in the middle of the test program. Pan Am opposed this project on the point of policy that nothing should delay the test and certification program and on the operational consideration that the test engines were not sufficiently reliable until the properly heat-treated pins could be produced. Boeing did not accept either objection and insisted that 747s could not be sold to enough foreign airlines until European governments and their airlines could see the airplane in flight, and escort many thousand potential European passengers through its impressive interior. Boeing convinced the FAA that U. S. prestige and leadership would be threatened if the 747 were not in Paris where the Concorde would make its first public flights. Eventually Pan Am insisted that 747 Number Four, on which Pan Am had made down payments approaching ten million dollars, should wear Pan Am's paint pattern if it were to be flown to Paris with FAA sanction. Boeing's response was prompt and clear to the effect that they were not about to try to sell to foreign airlines a 747 with Pan Am's exterior paint pattern as well as the Pan Am interior with which Number Four was already equipped. Since Boeing's 747 Number One had no interior furniture or fixtures, it could not be used as an effective sales model. Finally Boeing painted Number Four in a Boeing pattern, took Mr. Wilson, Mr. Boullioun, and their sales staffs to Paris non-stop from Seattle and, with no question, stole the spotlight at the Paris air show from the Concorde.

Pan Am did not passively accept Boeing's insistence that the visit to Paris should have no Pan Am flavor. For very many years Pan Am had a large staff in Paris and Boeing had almost none. Pan Am had developed relations with French officials and the French media which Boeing did not possess. As a result, in Paris when foreign governmental and airline authorities were invited to visit the 747, Pan Am representatives escorted them. When the public trooped through the airplane, Pan Am stewardesses guided them. Radio, TV, and press, without exception, described the "Pan Am airplane" although the pictures of the exterior showed a Boeing paint pattern rather than the well known Pan Am blue and white. Since the flight was made without incident, the net result was helpful to both Pan Am and Boeing. Pan Am had decided that there would be more important and costly arguments to win before accepting the first airplane than to go to court or otherwise force Boeing to put Pan Am paint on 747 Number Four for display at the Paris Air Show.

49 Days of Controversy Over Delivery and Acceptance. In October 1969, it became apparent that tests would be completed later than planned and the FAA certificate would not be awarded in time to meet Pan Am's plans to initiate operations and capture the European market before Christmas.

The growing delays in the flight test program and certification schedule generated another series of Pan Am - Boeing staff conflicts or controversies. To Boeing, the delays were disappointing and expensive. The fixes called for by new airframe "bugs" were in themselves expensive, and in fact each day's delay in the delivery of each airplane delayed Boeing's receipt of the almost ten million dollars which was the final half of the cost of each airplane and which was payable on delivery. As delays built up, the interest cost of such huge sums per airplane began eating into Boeing's planned profits.

For Pan Am, the delays were becoming increasingly costly and exasperating. In accordance with the delivery schedule in the contract, Pan Am had prepared to carry on intensive training in two provisionally certificated 747NPs in September and October, 1969. Pan Am intended to put two fully certificated 747Ns into commercial operation in November and add three more "Ns" in December and thereby capture the cream of the lucrative holiday traffic from the major terminals of the North Atlantic. That was one of the primary returns expected by Pan Am as a result of having pioneered the 747 program and having agreed to pay some two hundred and forty million dollars in early '69, six months before the scheduled delivery of that first training 747. Following immediately behind that introduction, Pan Am had planned to introduce three or four more 747s into commercial service per month and have all twenty-three fully operational by the end of May 1970 and thus be in firm position to reap the returns expected for the first summer tourist season into Europe, Asia, South America, and around-the-world. Elaborate plans to stand down senior 707 and DC-8 crews for 747 training, to reschedule 707s and DC-8s into less productive routes, plans to sell certain 707s and DC-8s which would be rendered surplus, and plans to advertise and promote the 747 with travel agents would all obviously suffer radical and expensive revision caused by breaches in contractual delivery schedules.

It was also evident in October that the first twenty or thirty 747s would be finished and tendered for delivery before Pratt & Whitney could begin producing JT9D-3 engines modified to correct ovalizing and pin failures. Without question Boeing would proffer delivery of resultant subspecification airplanes to Pan Am and probably one or two other airlines early on the delivery schedule. The alert and inquisitive financial and aviation press was already asking Pan Am what would happen when Boeing proposed to deliver aircraft with much higher fuel consumption and much less reliability than that which Pan Am had contracted to buy. Controversy was inevitable.

Pan Am Proposes that Boeing Pay Up. Pan Am fired the first gun in this new controversy in the form of a terse business message on 24 October 1969 in which Pan Am said, in brief, that if Pan Am accepted any 747s that could not meet specifications, Pan Am would insist that Boeing remedy those shortcomings at Boeing's expense on a firmly expedited schedule and additionally Boeing would reimburse Pan Am for all losses attributed to subspecification performance including costs of excess fuel, added flight time, and loss of revenue due to decreased payloads on long flights, all losses caused by airplane down-time attributed to engine change and modification, and all expenses related to delayed deliveries and markets missed. Boeing was again reminded that Pan Am had never failed to meet its contractual requirements to make advance payments.

On the same day an official letter was mailed to Boeing which quoted Boeing's telegram of 1 July in which they forecast the delivery to Pan Am of two training 747s in August and also Boeing's telegram of 16 October which forecast the delivery of the first of these two in the first week of November. This Pan Am letter added weight to claims for financial losses due to last minute but substantial delays in deliveries. These two papers initiated forty-nine days of intense staff meetings, conferences, and confrontations and all manner of outside pressures and battles of nerves. The problem was not settled until after an hour and a quarter on the telephone between the two presidents. This call was completed at seven fifteen PM Eastern Standard Time Friday evening December 12, 1969.

After the 24 October wire and letter, the now familiar negotiators met at Seattle on November 5th and 6th. Boeing presented a detailed review of the current status of airplane and engine programs and plans for future modifications and changes. The two teams then squared off on the basic purpose of the meeting—the terms under which Pan Am would accept subspecification 747s. From conversations in Seattle it appeared that Boeing had not taken seriously the relatively low level but nevertheless official Pan Am wire and letter of 24 October. It was then made very very clear that those were

September 1968–December 1969

the views of the Corporation and those were amplified by the further statement that Pan Am proposed to pay only fifty percent of the final payment due on delivery and to pay the balance as progress payments geared to Boeing's progress in remedying each of the shortcomings, all at Boeing's expense, of course. At this point Mr. Boullioun and his staff did take the Pan Am position seriously, and he asked for a recess until he could talk to Mr. Allen.

Pan Am Proposes to Pay Less. About three PM the conference reconvened on the somber note that Pan Am's fifty percent withholding, which would exceed four million dollars, upon the delivery of each airplane, with other customers presumably following suit, could bankrupt the Boeing Company. The argument was again advanced that Boeing could not be charged for delays which were caused by Pratt & Whitney. That argument was again countered with the fact that the contract for the airplane with engines and other accessories as selected by Boeing was a contract between Boeing and Pan American. The terms of Pratt & Whitney's contract with Boeing were outside the ken of Pan American. Then in lieu of Pan Am's partial payment proposal Mr. Boullioun offered a mixed bag of concessions. He offered to provide twenty-five kits with which Pan Am's 710,000 pound 747s could be converted to 747s authorized to take off at a weight of 735,000 pounds. This increase of some ten tons in permissible load per airplane per flight would, he contended, generously reimburse Pan Am for the temporary initial economic losses due to delays and engine deficiencies. He also offered Boeing's assurance to bring all deficiencies up to specification levels at Boeing's expense. In a subsequent Halaby-Kuter telephone conference, it was concluded that Pan Am would acknowledge the Boullioun concessions as small steps in the right direction, propose to accept them, and then reduce the amount withheld from each final payment on subspecification aircraft from fifty percent to thirty-five percent of the balance due. This counterproposal was not accepted by Boeing and the discussion remained stalemated until early December. There were almost daily contacts at technical levels, but no progress was made toward breaking the stalemate.

Flying Interlude—Mr. Halaby Wrings Out the 747. On the afternoon of November 7th, Mr. Halaby landed at Boeing Field in a Fan-Jet Falcon from Los Angeles where he had been attending to some other business. The purpose of his visit was to make his first flight in a 747. General Kuter had flown the 747 on earlier occasions but only briefly and not through any radical or testing maneuvers. Mr. Halaby had been a test pilot in the U.S. Navy not too many years previously and had kept his jet transport pilot qualifications current while flying the FAA administrative jets and the Fan Jet Falcons, the sales of which had been one of his earlier responsibilities in Pan Am.

Aboard 747 Number Four with Mr. Halaby were General Kuter and most of the members of the Pan Am negotiating team. Also aboard were Boeing's chief test pilot, several members of the FAA test crew, Mr. Boullioun, and most of the members of the Boeing negotiating team. The Boeing chief test pilot put Mr. Halaby at the left hand or captain's controls, talked to him throughout engine start, equipment check, taxi-out, take off, flight, and landings, but never touched the controls. On this, his first flight in the 747, Mr. Halaby took off, climbed to about 14,000 feet, and circled Mt. Ranier several times to check the 747's reaction to the turbulence one always finds around mountain tops. He then climbed to altitude and put this huge airplane through several full stalls, with and without power. At the top of exceedingly steep pull-ups, the whole airplane would shudder and shake, the huge wing flaps would buffet heavily in the condition of dead stall, the wing tips would wave up and down twelve feet or so and the airplane would finally fall forward in a whip-stall, wind up in a moderate dive dead ahead until flying speed was regained and then nose up to a normal flying posture. He flew the airplane on three engines and then with two engines dead on the same side. Finally he made several landings and take-offs on an abandoned air strip at Moses Lake, one of which included a three engine take-off and landing. The flight had many of the aspects of a test flight for a high speed military jet fighter. It was made by a one-time test pilot, but a pilot who had never before been in a 747 in flight. 747 Number Four was the fully outfitted 747 which the FAA was testing to prove safety and suitability for passenger service. All in all, the flight was convincing evidence that the Boeing engineers had built into the 747 all of the features that their accumulated wisdom and experience could devise to provide a strong and sturdy airplane, easy to fly and easy to handle under conditions many times more severe than would ever be encountered in commercial operations. Even to the experienced airline and manufacturing talent aboard, it was reassuring to observe safety characteristics in the 747 which were quite superior to characteristics of the predecessor 707s and DC-8s, which themselves were daily setting new safety records. For example, most jet airplanes, military and civil, when falling into a dive after a dead stall are inclined to fall off on one wing as if to begin a tail-spin. As they begin to pick up speed in their dive they tend to "tuck-under" and dive steeper and steeper. These normal jet characteristics are not dangerous but they require experienced pilots to keep them from becoming so. On the other hand, the 747 is designed to self-correct for all of those tendencies. When the 747 falls into a dive it falls dead ahead, not off on one wing. As it picks up speed it tends to level out, not to tuck-under into steeper dives. Those are examples of the safety that wise and experienced aeronautical engineers built into the 747.

War of Nerves—Again. During the stalemate in the discussion of the terms under which Pan Am would accept the first 747s, both sides used all the pressures that were available to the negotiators. After repeated statements that Pan Am would let those first airplanes sit and by implication tie up all other deliveries until acceptable terms were offered, Boeing developed some procedures which they said their lawyers approved to tender aircraft for delivery to subsequent customers if Pan Am refused to accept the initial tenders. From the Boeing factory, news leaked to the effect that TWA had plans for a twenty-four hour conversion of their training 747 to a configuration the FAA could certify as suitable for passengers and thereby preempt Pan Am's cherished and contractual Number One position.

On the 20th of November, test airplane Number Five in full TWA paint pattern was cleared by Boeing for Hawaii with the claim that FAA tests required landings and take-offs from a high temperature airdrome. General Kuter telephoned Mr. Boullioun and stated that Pan Am was furious at this patent attempt to associate TWA with the first 747 flight into the Pacific, particularly in view of Boeing's refusal to put the Pan Am paint pattern on Number Four's flight to Paris. Pan Am cited the availability of many high temperature airdromes located in our southwest desert areas. Mr. Boullioun radioed instructions to Number Five to turn around half way to Hawaii and return to Seattle.

On the Pan Am side, with perhaps more subtlety than courtesy, Boeing was asked if they wished to collaborate on the statement Pan Am would have to give to the press if the first airplane to be tendered was not acceptable.

September 1968–December 1969

A crack appeared in the stalemate after the long Thanksgiving weekend holiday at the Boeing plant when on the first day of December Boeing's president, Mr. T. Wilson, entered the negotiations through his long telephone call to the Pan Am president, Mr. Najeeb Ialaby. The Pan Am staff had prepared for Mr. Halaby a note to the effect that Pan Am's negotiating position would never be stronger with Boeing than while discussing acceptance of the first airplane. The press and notably the Wall Street Journal were asking Pan Am what they would do about accepting substandard airplanes and engines. Certain Pan Am stockholders were vocally critical of Pan Am management. All considerations pointed to Pan Am's making a strong stand. The staff then summarized all open items in the controversy with Boeing as three major items and a number of lesser items. In order that there be no misunderstanding between companies at top level, Mr. Halaby enumerated and outlined Pan Am's position on each of these open items to Mr. Wilson. Mr. Wilson took notes and said that he would study them.

On the next day Boeing flew Number Four, still in Boeing paint pattern, to New York presumably for a "fit check" against Pan Am's ground handling equipment and brought a large group of aviation press writers along. Boeing permitted Pan Am to nominate about 50% of the guests on this flight. Mr. Allen and Mr. Boullioun were aboard. That night they invited Mr. Halaby and General Kuter for another dinner conference in a private room of the St. Regis. Again Mr. Halaby enumerated and supported each of the open items. Again Mr. Allen rejected all of them.

To counter Mr. Allen's argument that withholding some four million dollars from the final payment on each airplane for the weeks or months needed to bring them up to specification would bankrupt Boeing, Mr. Halaby observed that the interest on $4,000,000 if applied to every one of the first thirty airplanes would be less than one percent of Boeing's total write-offs for the development costs of the 747 for the current year.

Arguments in detail, point by point, continued until the conference broke up at midnight with agreement on no single point. It was evident that the staff deadlocks had become deadlocks between chief executives as well. This war of nerves had also reached the highest corporate levels.

A real break in the deadlock occurred the next morning. Mr. Allen participated in some flights in 747 Number Four from JFK airport with airline officials who had ordered none or few 747s and Mr. Boullioun spent the morning in General Kuter's office. They proceeded to draft compromises on many of the points at issue which they felt might be acceptable to their Chief Executives. For example, the proportion of the final payments which Pan Am had proposed to withhold on the first deliveries might be reduced and Pan Am would further reduce it by increasing the estimated cash value of the earlier "fixes" that Boeing might achieve on subsequent deliveries. While some softening was evident in Boeing's proposals for compromise in lieu of flat rejection, negotiations had not softened in tone. Outside pressures were still in effect. Mr. Boullioun learned by telephone from Seattle that Pan Am had withdrawn its flight crew which had been awaiting instructions at Pan Am's office in the Boeing factory to take delivery and fly away the first 747. Mr. Boullioun dropped the word that TWA was planning demonstration flights in the New York area by its training 747 on December 12th.

Late on December 3rd Mr. Boullioun told General Kuter that he had long telephone conferences with his people in Seattle and was ready to give a little more on most of the open items. General Kuter applauded these moves as small steps in the right direction and reduced Pan Am's demands proportionately. The gaps had been narrowed but were far from closed. That night Mr. Allen left for Seattle aboard 747 Number Four. Mr. Boullioun remained in New York to carry on the negotiations.

On December 4th there were many staff telephone conferences and Mr. Boullioun also spent considerable time on the telephone with Seattle while General Kuter kept an all day engagement with a large visiting party on an annual visit to Pan Am from the Industrial College of the Armed Forces. That night he explained to Mr. Boullioun that the Pan Am staff would be involved all day Friday, December 5th, in a Quarterly Management Review scheduled to begin at 9:30 AM. General Kuter agreed to meet with Mr. Boullioun well before the offices normally opened in the Pan Am Building.

During a very busy hour early on December 5th, Mr. Boullioun announced his agreement to a large number of technical and relatively minor open items related to the acceptance of the first airplane and some very small improvements in Bocing's offers to meet Pan Am's major points. He departed with the statement that he must leave for a conference in TWA's headquarters in Kansas City and that, if Pan Am still stood firm, Boeing would tender on December 8th the first Pan Am airplane for delivery on December 11th. If Pan Am would not accept delivery on December 11th, all of Boeing's concessions would be withdrawn and settlements would have to be sought by court action. Even between good friends there was no armistice in this war of nerves.

Late on December 5th General Kuter called Mr. Boullioun in the office of Mr. Parmet, Vice-President TWA in Kansas City. He observed that further progress toward agreement depended primarily on Boeing's substantial increase in the amount of payment which they agreed might be withheld until discrepancies were remedied. General Kuter emphasized "substantial." Except for agreements on the working of the technical and minor matters in the negotiations, there were no further developments until the date which Boeing had set to tender legally for delivery the first airplane, December 8, 1969.

Late that day Mr. Wilson telephoned Mr. Halaby. In New York, General Kuter was in Mr. Halaby's office with interoffice communications with the other members of the negotiation team. In Seattle, Mr. Wilson apparently had Mr. Boullioun and others with him. Mr. Halaby established a rock bottom figure as the sum he would have to withhold from the final payments to satisfy his stockholders that Pan Am's payments were reduced in exact proportion to the reduced performance of the aircraft being bought. Mr. Wilson seemed to be surprised to learn that Pan Am would agree to schemes to graduate the balance of the payments with the separate improvements that Boeing had agreed to make and that Pan Am would make those payments as promptly as each improvement was accomplished. Furthermore, both Pan Am and Boeing believed that all improvements would be incorporated in the production line by the time Pan Am's twelfth airplane was completed. The full contract price would be paid for the first airplane which would meet specified performance upon delivery. Pan Am was surprised that Mr. Wilson was willing to discuss Mr. Halaby's substantial rock-bottom withholding. Both agreed that the two staffs should try to produce an acceptable scheme for the progressive payments of the substantial amount to be withheld.

Late that night from home General Kuter called Mr. Boullioun and they confirmed their mutual understandings as to the further work to be done by the staffs in concert. General Kuter made no reference to the fact that that was the scheduled date to proffer the first airplane. Mr. Boullioun introduced the subject and volunteered to defer the proffer of delivery of the critical first airplane for one day. Pan Am's delivery crew had been withdrawn from Seattle. The war of nerves was not dead, although the subject of a formal tender was never again raised. Some contentious points developed as the many people involved on both sides tried to produce legal wording in a mutually acceptable delivery document. On December tenth both staffs passed upward identical statements of the points on which agreements could not be reached.

Using these as notes, Mr. Halaby and Mr. Wilson reviewed them by telephone on 11 December and reached a common understanding as to what the differences were in actuality. During these days, Pan Am was advised through several sources in Seattle of TWA plans to usurp Pan Am's cherished position of being "first with the 747" particularly in the New York market. At all echelons Pan Am stood fast on all points of policy.

At six PM Eastern Standard Time on 12 December Mr. Wilson again called Mr. Halaby. Using the notes of the previous day Mr. Wilson discussed each point from the least important to the most, conceding on the least and suggesting some modification on the most difficult points. Mr. Halaby concluded that his rock-bottom figure had pressed Boeing as far as the Boeing management dared go. The two Chief Executives outlined the substance of the further agreements to be spelled out by the lawyers and the negotiating teams. At about 7:30 PM they exchanged a figurative hand-shake as Mr. Wilson told his people to deliver the first 747 to Pan Am, and Mr. Halaby told his people to write the check, less his substantial rock-bottom withholding, and accept the airplane.

That night the Pan Am delivery crew moved from its base in San Francisco. The next morning they accepted the airplane, flew a load of cargo to Nassau non-stop, and then moved to the Pan Am facility at the JFKennedy Airport in New York where *but nobody* would preempt Pan Am's being "First with the 747."

CHAPTER 4

747 Operations and Growth
January 1970–January 1972

Results of First Year of Operation

Crises Continue. With the delivery of Pan Am's first training airplane, the major contractual negotiations and bargaining came to an end, but crises involving Boeing and Pan Am were far from terminated. Each appeared to be timed to provide a "cliff-hanging" aspect to most of the major elements of the introduction and initiation of 747 operations. The christening of Pan Am's fully certificated airplane had been scheduled and publicized for January 15, 1970 at Dulles International Airport with Mrs. Nixon doing the honors. Two days earlier, a series of failures of the left rear emergency evacuation chute on some test airplanes caused the FAA to consider suspending the certification or prohibiting the series of daytime demonstration flights to which several hundred christening guests had been invited and to witness the christening. This "cliff hanger" was resolved at the last moment after a review of the earlier successful test operations of that one and all of the other nine chutes on this particular airplane. Additionally, Pan Am promised that all passengers would be seated in the areas of the many other emergency exits. Previous tests at night and with no lights had proved that only three chutes were needed to evacuate a fully loaded 747 within the allowed ninety seconds. This was an example not only of a cliff hanging crisis but also of the extreme lengths to which Pan Am, Boeing, and the FAA were going to avoid any degree of jeopardy to safety in bringing out the 747.

Pan Am's Plans to Initiate 747 Service. Almost all elements of the Pan Am staff started preliminary planning for the introduction of the 747s and the attendant revision of 707, DC-8, and 727 schedules as soon as Boeing's contractual delivery schedule was established in early 1966. By 1967 it had become necessary to coordinate interlocking plans for promotion, demonstration, and operation as they related to ground and air training, traffic potentials, airport preparation, availability of ground handling equipment, advertising, finance, international agreements, and the interests of the International Air Transport Association and the International Civil Aviation Organization. Vice-President Randolph W. Kirk, Ground Operations, had well over twenty years of Pan Am experience in Pan Am's Operations Department and on major overseas bases. Mr. Kirk also had natural capability as an overall planner. He was relieved of all other duties and was designated as the coordinator and planner for the introduction of the 747. He reported directly to the Executive Vice-President.

In 1968 and 1969 Mr. Kirk's office walls were well covered with detailed PERT and PLANNET charts. Greatly compressed copies of these were on the desks of most of the senior officers of the company. The basic PLANNET Chart was dated 12/1/66. Its final revision was Number 8 dated 1/1/70. The Master Schedule covered Flight Operation, Ground Operation, Maintenance, Property and Facilities, and of course Finance. Each major schedule was broken down into all essential elements of detail. The Flight Operations Plan, for example, began with the selection, purchase, and installation of a 747 Simulator (itself a multimillion dollar training device not yet invented in 1966); the selection of 747 instructor and operating flight crews as well as a base for their training (a one time Strategic Air Command Base off the major airways at Roswell, New Mexico was finally selected); the development of flight manuals and procedures; the selection and training of 747 Dispatchers; and overall administration to control costs and to remain within budgets.

The Maintenance Program similarly had problems of site selection for jet engine test cells several times larger than Pan Am had ever before designed and built; the provisioning of as yet undeveloped sets of airplane and engine spare parts; and extensive training procedures still to be developed. Flight Service Programs had to be coordinated in time with all others and Flight Service specialists were needed to participate in the design of the 747 interior, particularly its galleys, bars and components; design and locate commissaries, kitchens and food handling equipment; design and procure trays, china, glassware; even the meal patterns, menus, and wine cards. All these plans had to be accomplished at the time acceptable to sales, advertising, and public relations. The Property and Facilities Program for the global operations of the 747 was an enormous one, involving huge terminals and massive facilities at main bases at Los Angeles and at JFK in New York. Lesser but vital facilities had to be considered at about thirty other airports, most of which were in foreign countries.

The problem of keeping these broad spread, overlapping, and complicated programs coordinated was made especially difficult by their continually changing nature. Each delay in Boeing's delivery schedule, for example, would cause the sales staff to reevaluate the demands for passenger service throughout the world and frequently revise tentative schedules as the demands of the market changed with the seasons. Such a change would then call for facilities at bases at changed times. In like manner a relatively minor change in one program might cause major repercussions in others as red flags appeared in the PLANNET Charts on the walls of the Kirk office.

First Commercial Flight. After roll-out, first test flight, FAA certification, and the official christening, the next critical event in the history of the 747, or in the case of any of its predecessors, was its first commercial flight or its actual entry into the business of air transportation. In Pan Am there had never been any question as to where the first 747 would go into operation. Flight No. 2, the overnight flight from New York to London, which was also the first leg of the east-bound round-the-world flight, had always been heavily patronized. It, combined with Flight No. 101, a day time west-bound flight from London to New York, represented the best money-making combination of Pan Am schedules that could be operated by one airplane. The round trip called for a six to six and a half hour flight eastbound, a three hour and twenty minute layover and, into the prevailing westerly winds, a return flight of seven to seven and a half hours which would be finally followed by a seven to eight hour layover. That combination of schedules provided daily utilization of thirteen to fourteen hours with reasonable time for maintenance and cleaning, all of which was an ideal money making arrangement for a single 747 or a 707.

When Mr. Gray was Chief Executive, it was planned to initiate the "2-101" schedule as soon as the first certificated 747 was available. The Technical Staff had argued that the schedule should not be started until a second 747 was on hand to serve as "cover." They argued that the new and untried nature of the airplane, its many new accessories, and particularly its new engines made it unlikely that everything would work smoothly enough to guarantee a reliable thirteen to fourteen hour daily utilization at the outset and the conspicuous first 747 should not be exposed to a reputation of irregularity or unreliability. On the other hand, Mr. Gray knew that Pan Am had been overly cautious in its initial 707 schedules and allowed competitors to capture some early business. He knew that a fully loaded 747 on Flight No. 2 out to London and Flight No. 101 back could produce over two and a half million dollars a month in revenue and he decided not to miss any of those highly remunerative first days. After Mr. Gray turned over the responsibility of Chief Executive to Mr. Halaby, the staff's more conservative recommendation prevailed and it was thereafter planned to schedule the initial operation on Flights Nos. 2 - 101 when two 747s with unrestricted FAA certificates were on hand and available. One would be set up to operate and the other would be held as cover for that flight when there was any doubt that the scheduled airplane would be ready. When the second airplane was not required for cover, it was to be used for training until a full complement of trained crews was available. Thereafter the cover airplane could be scheduled for the shorter routes from New York. The cover airplane, for example, could easily take-off with a big load for Puerto Rico after the London Flight No. 2 had departed and return to JFK from Puerto Rico long before the Flight No. 101 could return from London.

Uncertain Boeing Production Schedule. Originally the contract called for the delivery of the first two fully certificated 747s in November of 1969. These dates were the basis for initial plans until September 22, 1969 when Boeing promised delivery of the second 747 in the "first half of January, 1970." While the two months slippage in a three and a half year schedule cannot be viewed as any great failure, it caused widespread anguish to some of the Pan Am sales and advertising staff who had already placed advertising formats in the hands of the media and who had always claimed that a full year was needed to market a product as new as 747 travel.

Visits to the factory and assurances by the men doing the work convinced the Pan Am staff that a second or a "cover" 747 would actually be on hand to support a first commercial flight on January 15, 1970. Mr. Halaby sounded out degrees of confidence in that forecast and decided to release advertisements and publicity for the first commercial flight as Pan Am Flight No. 2 to take-off at 1900 hours Wednesday, 21 January 1970.

"The 747 Inaugural Flight is Loading at Gate One." Of the many hundreds of applicants for that first flight, a representative blue ribbon component of three hundred and thirty-two passengers and an excited crew of twenty were hand-picked for that first flight with Captain Robert M. Weeks, Pan Am's chief 747 instructor pilot at the controls. Although that first flight was completed to London, to the Pan Am and Boeing authorities who had nursed the 747 from inception, their hoped for "dream flight" had more of the aspects of a nightmare. The three hundred and thirty-two passengers took their flight and its alterations in carnival spirit. The staffs took it as an operational fiasco. The press exploited all adverse aspects and increased their death-watch numbers and vigilance at JFK.

The facts of the first flight, while far from rosy, represented bad luck more than bad management. No one was surprised that the take-off was delayed by twenty-five minutes. The improvised 747 terminal at JFK was flooded with many hundreds there to see the three hundred and thirty-two passengers depart, many hundreds more came to look at the famous 747, and there were still many more spectators who just happened to be at the airport.

Of the twenty crew members, more than half of the cabin crew had never before been inside a real 747, few had ever flown in a 747, and none had ever served a paying passenger in a 747. Their training had been in mock-up interiors.

As Captain Weeks and his flight engineer started up their four new JT9D engines and slowly taxied out down wind to the take-off position, a question as to the airplane's "load-and-balance" status caused the flight engineer to check into his papers, temporarily taking his eyes away from his critical instrument panel. At that instant a gust of tail wind into the rear exhaust of the big jet engine caused it to flare back and overheat. No one saw the overheat signal or took any immediate corrective action, so this condition was permitted to generate heat which exceeded allowable limits. As soon as this was recognized, and with only partially concealed disappointment, Captain Weeks took the safe and conservative course of action; he shut down the engine that had overheated and announced to his inaugural crew and passengers that they were returning to the line for a maintenance check.

"The 747 Inaugural Flight is Unloading at Gate One." The maintenance chief opened up the cowling around the problem engine but could see no evidence of damage. Nevertheless, he concluded that parts would have to be put through metallurgical laboratory tests to be perfectly sure that there had been no damaging overheating. It just happened that Mr. Gwinn and Mr. Smith, Chief Executives of United Aircraft and Pratt & Whitney, were among the three hundred and thirty-two passengers on this flight.

The maintenance chief estimated that a satisfactory engine change at about midnight with an inexperienced ground crew might take longer than the time required to change over to the stand-by 747. Consequently the stand-by airplane was taken off its training flight and was taxied up to the terminal. The galleys of the scheduled airplane were unloaded and transferred to the stand-by. All passenger service items were moved from one airplane to the other, baggage was transferred, and a new clearance for the flight was obtained. Meanwhile the stewardesses and the passenger service staff at JFK were very busy entertaining, wining, and dining three hundred and thirty-two passengers as guests through the slowly moving midnight hours. The press was interviewing delayed passengers including Mr. Gwinn and Mr. Smith but they were finding more holiday spirit than carping criticism. The fact that Pan Am included the press in thirst quenching and dining along with the very important passengers also eased some potentially adverse writing.

"The 747 Inaugural Flight is Loading at Gate One, Again." Finally, six hours late, Pan Am Flight No. 2 taxied out again. The crossing of the Atlantic was smooth but all Europe knew that the inaugural 747, Pan Am Flight No. 2 had suffered a long delay and was five and a half hours late on its first scheduled arrival at London.

Back in New York, when the safe arrival message of the first flight was received, Pan Am executives assured themselves that operations and maintenance authorities were making every possible effort to get the second flight off on time, then at last they could go to bed, well over six hours late.

On the second day, on January 22, Flight No. 2 had 237 passengers, 3666 pounds of mail, and 1495 kilograms of cargo aboard. It was scheduled to leave the blocks at 1900 hours. It left at 1902 hours. On the 23rd of January it left at 1905, the 24th at 1901, the 25th at 1901 and until February 11th when bad weather in Europe caused a delay of one hour and fifty minutes and eventual diversion into Frankfurt, Germany, the 747s which were flying Pan Am Flight No. 2 averaged two minutes and twenty seconds late in scheduled time off the blocks at JFK. Thirty-six minutes was the longest delay and nine trips were off the blocks exactly on schedule. This record was superior to any on-time effort Pan Am had ever made with any previous new-type airplane. This record was one which even the crews that made it had trouble believing for they were still reading press reviews of the delay and unreliability demonstrated on the first day of these first three weeks. The details of timely performance after that first day got scant attention from the press.

Teething Problems. Vice-President Kirk presented a detailed review of the first thirty days of operation on 20 February 1970. Only four Pan Am Flights had been operated with the 747s that had been available. Flights No. 2 and No. 101 to and from London and Flights Nos. 271 and 292 to and from San Juan, Puerto Rico. "On time" records were good but were due, in part, to the use of one 747 as a cover airplane. However in the case of "2 - 101," the "on time" record was marred by bad winter weather in Europe. Several eastbound 747s were diverted from London to Frankfurt. By the time weather permitted them to move from Frankfurt to London, they were too late to permit on-time departures for New York. Two malicious false bomb warnings on the Puerto Rico flight caused long delays as passengers were evacuated and the huge baggage and cargo containers were searched. The cover 747N at JFK was used for training when it was not needed to maintain a schedule. It and the two 747NP training airplanes at Roswell, New Mexico had produced eighty-one qualified 747 pilots by 17 February 1970. These included eight Chief Pilots, seven Flight Instructors, thirty Pan Am Captains, twenty Pan Am First Officers, twelve American Airlines Pilots, and four Inspector Pilots. When Pan Am agreed to lease two 747s to American Airlines, it also agreed to put American Airlines crews through the Pan Am training courses.

The Baggage Problem. Baggage delivery varied with the types of passengers and the facilities at terminals. At San Juan on the arrival of Flight No. 271, the time from the arrival of the first passenger in the baggage claim area until the last bag was available for claim ran from a low of seventeen minutes to a high of thirty-three minutes. On flights from San Juan to JFK, the same times ran from twenty-seven to forty-four minutes. When Flight No. 101 arrived at JFK the times were three to thirty minutes, and for Flight No. 2 the times were two to thirty-four minutes. Major efforts were made to reduce the time passengers had to wait for baggage.

The serious blunders of the first thirty days were studied and precautions taken against repetition. The requirement for exact control of the large enclosed baggage containers was learned the hard way. Passengers on the first 747 that was diverted to Frankfurt were moved to their proper destinations on 707s. Their baggage was taken from the large containers in the 747 and transferred to the 707s. Unfortunately one loaded container with sixty bags was overlooked in the baggage transfer process. Since the closed containers looked alike, loaded or unloaded, the error was not detected until hours later. Forty irate passengers at different points in Europe did not receive their sixty pieces of luggage till late that night. A new system of opening all baggage containers was installed immediately. Flight Service was slow, passengers were congesting the aisles, waste disposal was inadequate, and the newly designed color projectors for the in-flight movies were far from satisfactory.

The Learning Curve. Pan Am, Boeing, and Pratt & Whitney engineers were scrutinizing every flight to detect and if possible to anticipate the "bugs" that would inevitably show up in early regularly scheduled heavy operation. Pan Am's Chief Engineer, Mr. John G. Borger, on January 29th reported six pages of 747 discrepancies which varied in severity from faulty passenger reading lights to an increasing rate of engine failures. Some discrepancies were little more than nuisances but still severely handicapped schedule reliability. An example was the compressed air bottles which were installed to assist the flight stewardesses in opening the heavy main doors in an emergency. The lever that activated that bottle and helped open the door and then ejected and inflated the emergency evacuation chute on the 747 looked very much like the lever that steadied the door of the 707 after it had been opened. Twice partially trained and over-eager stewardesses activated the air bottle inadvertently. Twice the huge chutes deployed on transient airports where there were no facilities to repack the chutes and at first there were no replacements. Twice flights with hundreds of passengers were delayed for hours by this discrepancy.

Other discrepancies were related to accessories. An example was an unacceptable failure rate of the Auxiliary Power Unit mounted high in the tail of the 747. The failure of such an additional source of electric power might not seem to be serious. While it did not jeopardize safety, its failure did cause delays. Among other functions, it provided power to operate the air conditioning system when the airplane was on the ground and the engines were not running. It also provided power to start the big JT9Ds at airports where out-sized ground power units were not at hand. Because of the size of the airplane and engines, the APU was a specially designed jet turbine which generated more power than any of the main engines which flew, and still fly, the DC-3.

All inspectors, airlines, manufacturers, and FAA were intense in their search for discrepancies that jeopardized safety. In ninety days Mr. Borger's six page list of fifty-seven discrepancies was reduced to four pages with sixteen discrepancies.

This search continues, of course, through the service life of all types of civil commercial air transports.

Political and Competitive Obstacles. Additional problems were generated from political or competitive sources. Mr. Forrest Cloud (Bud) Wiser, Jr., the President of TWA, made two public statements which disparaged the flying qualities of the 747. His observation that the 747 flew like a "lead sled" was given wide press coverage. Mr. Wiser was an ex-airline pilot who had a short time at the controls of a 747 but did not put it through vigorous paces as Mr. Halaby had. Mr. Halaby had praised its flying qualities and repeated his studied conclusion after Mr. Wiser's public disparagement. The active and current TWA pilots who had flown the 747 were fully as enthusiastic about its flying qualities as were the Pan Am pilots. It was speculated that Mr. Wiser's comments might have been motivated by competitive considerations. TWA's certificated 747s followed well behind Pan Am's in the delivery schedules and Mr. Wiser was not happy in watching Pan Am working to capture the 747 market across the North Atlantic. Also he was not happy with Boeing's response to TWA's negotiations concerning their delayed deliveries and subspecification performance. The Wiser comment slowly faded into the broad background of past press problems.

One cliff-hanging delay attended Pan Am's initiation of 747 flights into Paris and Rome on the first of March. It was anticipated that there might be political objections to Pan Am's preempting markets at Orly and in Rome before the state-owned and -controlled airlines Air France and Alitalia received their 747s. Such had happened when Pan Am initiated 707 operations. Unhappily the FAA had published elaborate air traffic Notices To Airmen (NOTAMs) concerning the possibility that there might be something special about the "wake" of the 747 in flight and its jet-blast on the airport.

FAA also issued guidance or directives to keep other aircraft separated in flight from the 747s by several times the amount of normal separation. This created great problems in the already congested airspace around Paris and elsewhere. On the 26th of February, Pan Am's Director for France, Mr. Kent Fry in Paris had word from French authorities that they might not clear the 747 into France until hazard of the alleged wake was reduced or eliminated. There were rumblings of similar concern in Rome and even in London where the 747 was already operating. By telephone from Paris to New York and later with Pan Am, Boeing, and FAA authorities in Washington, the FAA finally explained to the French authorities that the extensive testing of the 747 and C5A along with the 707, DC-8, and 727 on instrumented ranges at Edwards Air Force Base in the Mojave Desert had proved that the "wash" from the 747 was little if any more vigorous than the "wash" that had been experienced for ten years from the 707 and DC-8 and accommodated without trouble. At the last moment, Pan Am's 747 was cleared for operations into Orly.

Boeing was squarely in the middle of a threatened suit by a major customer in mid February. Pan Am had contracted to lease two early 747s to American Airlines with which American could initiate coast-to-coast domestic airline service before TWA could do so. Because the terms of the lease were highly remunerative to Pan Am and American Airlines' domestic services would not harm Pan Am's international business, this lease was important to Pan Am. American Airlines' early entry into domestic service would in fact help Pan Am by pinning some of TWA's later aircraft to transcontinental service rather than leaving them free to operate over international routes which competed with Pan Am. For those same reasons, the lease infuriated TWA, which talked of suing Boeing for permitting Pan Am to make the lease. While not at all anxious to aggravate TWA, another important customer, Boeing had to explain that they had no jurisdiction over the uses to which Pan Am might put any 747s after they were delivered and paid for.

Pan Am's Intramural Competitions. Mr. Kirk's office, then General Kuter's, and occasionally Mr. Halaby's were the scenes of some vigorous differences of views within the Pan Am staff concerning the promotion and the introduction of the 747. From inception there had been requirements to judge between Engineering and Marketing on items of passenger appeal and comfort. Marketing wanted the most luxurious seats, the widest aisles, the roomiest galleys, and in all cases the most appealing and saleable passenger comforts. Engineering pointed out that one unnecessary pound of weight in each seat would reduce the payload and revenue of the airplane by the equivalent of two passengers. Similarly, any galley that was larger than actually required for average loads would increase the airplane weight still more and also consume space that might be used for saleable seats. Finance entered most of these staff problems, particularly where seats varied in cost from around five hundred dollars each to over fifteen hundred dollars each, and Pan Am was buying almost four hundred seats for each airplane.

A most strenuous staff competition grew out of the question of the proportion of early 747 flying that should be diverted from revenue producing schedules to advertising and promotional purposes. On the day before Christmas 1969, Marketing and Public Relations were strongly supporting a detailed schedule which would move a fully crewed and equipped 747 into each airport served by Pan Am in the United States, Puerto Rico, and Hawaii and the major airports in Europe for promotional flying. A normal daily schedule would include two hours of static display for all local company employees and their families. There would be two one-hour courtesy flights for an especially invited list of about three hundred civic authorities, travel agents, and radio, TV, and press representatives on each flight. About three hours would be set up for thousands of the interested public to walk through the airplane; and, later that evening, the airplane, crew and the most important travel agents and media writers would take off for the next port of call where the program would begin early the next morning. All guests on such flights would be provided overnight accommodations and tickets to return home. Such a program was obviously very expensive. The Finance Department suggested that the 24 December promotion schedule was written by Santa Claus.

The amount of the capital investment on the twenty million dollar airplane and its ground service equipment could be computed and the operating expenses could be estimated. Every hour of flight, for example, consumed four thousand gallons of jet fuel. Every landing cost a fee which in some cases exceeded a thousand dollars. By the demands of the Airline Pilots Association, the captain might have to be paid an annual salary of $58,000 for some seventy-five hours flying per month. The Finance Department argued that Pan Am could not afford such avoidable expenses as those proposed for the elaborate introductory presentation to the public. Marketing estimated that the increased sales would produce a great net gain for Pan Am. Marketing couldn't support its arguments with facts, however.

Promotional flying was considerably reduced in scale and aircraft were so used only when they were not specifically required for training or for scheduled airline operation.

Delivery Schedules Still Slip. In April 1970, Pratt & Whitney were shipping slowly increasing numbers of modified JT9D-3 engines to Seattle for installation in new aircraft.

Boeing production was well ahead of Pratt & Whitney and many 747s without engines, known as "747 gliders," stood on the delivery ramp at Everett. Boeing was under tremendous pressure to install the few available modified engines by all airlines which had airplanes nearing completion. The smaller lines or those with few on order could argue disproportionate hardship in accepting unmodified engines, then going into operation, and shortly having to stand down to convert to modified engines. The Pan Am inspectors in the Boeing plant believed that Boeing was installing engines on 747 Production Line Number 51 scheduled for Japan Air Lines while Number 47, scheduled for June delivery as Pan Am's nineteenth airplane, stood by on the delivery ramp with no engines at all. On April 17th Mr. Halaby signed a letter to Mr. Allen which politely requested him to advance the date of delivery of Pan Am's nineteenth, twentieth, and twenty-first 747s from June to May and reminded him that the contract called for their delivery in April. His polite letter did not refer to the Pan Am treasurer's study which concluded that a one month delay in receipt of those three airplanes would reduce Pan Am's projected peak season profits by slightly over four and a half million dollars. A polite reply was wired a week later. Mr. Allen said that Boeing would try to expedite delivery if the Pan Am acceptance staff would get together and would cooperate with the Boeing staff. Four days later a less restrained wire from Mr. Halaby told Mr. Allen that the Pan Am staff had cooperated with the Boeing staff and accepted incomplete or imperfect aircraft except where safety was prejudiced and would continue to do so, confident that Boeing would continue to bring such aircraft up to standard as quickly as possible after delivery. He then referred to Boeing's contractual delivery dates and, without citing the apparent preferential treatment being given to JAL, said that Pan Am would not tolerate delayed deliveries on its big initial order while later and lesser orders were not equally delayed. Mr. Allen got the message although his response replayed the well worn contention that Boeing could not be responsible for delays caused by Pratt & Whitney. Pan Am's deliveries were speeded up. JAL's airplane did not step ahead of Pan Am's in the receiving line.

As the JT9D-3 modified engine delivery gained impetus, Boeing came closer to delivery schedules and by mid-summer Pan Am had received all twenty-five 747s. This number remained in operation until one airplane was sky-jacked to Cairo, Egypt, where it was evacuated and then destroyed by politically motivated criminals.

Pan Am Fleet Reworked. After the summer peak in 1970, Pan Am initiated another thirty million dollar project with Boeing, Pratt & Whitney, and several equipment suppliers. The twenty-four 747s were scheduled, two at a time, to return to the Boeing factory to be refurbished and modified in the light of all that was learned during the breaking-in and the teething periods. The refurbishing contract was designed to bring all improvements in "on-time" dependability, passenger service features, and economic performance up to the limits of the state-of-the-art in late 1970. Seventy-five percent of the cost of the rehabilitation fell on Boeing, Pratt & Whitney, and suppliers as a result of the Warranty Clauses which Vice-President Blackwell had been instrumental in incorporating in the initial contract for Pan Am.

By the end of the first full year of operation, January 20, 1971, five refurbished 747s were in operation and two more were in the process. Each of the five had new seat cushions and all evidence of the wear and tear of a busy first year of operation was removed. Each had been strengthened and had new FAA certificates which authorized the take-off weight to be increased from 712,000 to 735,000 pounds. This added capacity would add either 460 miles to the airplane's normal operating range or, alternatively, would add fifteen percent payload on flights up to 4,500 miles. This change promised substantial economic benefits. Interior modifications included galley changes to permit faster meal service, major improvements to the passenger entertainment system, the installation of even more soundproofing, and many improvements in the comfort and convenience of furniture and fixtures. By the summer of 1971, all the original twenty-four 747s were scheduled to be through modification and would be joined by eight more new aircraft to bring Pan Am's fleet to thirty-two 747 passenger aircraft.

System for the Seventies—A Success? Critics claimed that the 747 was too big and too early. As the unanticipated recession of 1970 reduced air travel, those critics became more strident and confident. Pan Am common stock skidded from a high of thirty-six to a low of eight. To pay for later 747s, Pan Am sold bonds but had to pay up to eleven and one quarter percent interest. Nevertheless on January 21, 1971, the anniversary of the first commercial flight, Pan Am pointed out that four and a half billion revenue passenger miles had been flown by Pan Am's initial 747s with a perfect safety record, a record which no other airplane in commercial aviation could equal. Pan Am was convinced that the 747 was the most efficient flying machine ever produced, that its operating costs were more than twenty percent less per seat mile than the money making 707, and happily had been contracted before inflation began to gallop. There was no question that Pan Am's capacity, after adding twenty-four 747s to its fleet, exceeded demand during the unforecast world recession of '69 and '70. This excess capacity was no great surprise to Pan Am as the 747 capacity was planned to meet the demands of the decade of the '70s. Such capacity naturally would be somewhat excessive in the earlier years, even without the worldwide recession. Pan Am had not anticipated that such a recession would result in so many unfilled seats in airplanes, so many empty hotel rooms, or such great difficulty in selling the older and less productive 707s and DC-8s rendered excess by the 747 capacities.

Pan Am and Boeing believed that the 747 would prove to be the foundation upon which a new structure of airline profitability would be built. While it will take time to confirm or deny such sweeping allegations, the facts of Pan Am's first year of operating the 747 offer little ammunition to pessimistic critics.

One million six hundred thousand people flew in Pan Am's 747s to twenty-two cities around the world, safely.

In addition to the passengers and their baggage, forty-two thousand seven hundred tons of air freight were handled in the first year of service.

The system-wide passenger load factor was fifty percent.

Fleet-wide, Pan Am's 747s flew an average of 9.5 hours daily toward the end of the first year.

In the first year of operation there were blunders and naturally many "bugs" were uncovered in the airplane, its engines, and accessories as well as in its maintenance, operation, and passenger service. The Pan Am records however indicate that there were fewer "bugs" than had been encountered in any previous major changes in aircraft. No "groundings" were required by the 747. Fleet-wide "groundings" had been directed on other aircraft. Pan Am maintains that all identified "bugs" have led to study and action to prevent their repetition and further to improve the service, reliability, and safety of the 747.

A prominent "bug" was encountered in the reaction of the passengers themselves, entitled by a Pan Am wag "the result of a Passenger Liberation Movement." The well advertised spaciousness in the 747 resulted in new and unexpected movements of passengers, walking in the aisles, stretching, visiting friends, and enjoying ample roominess, but meanwhile cluttering up the aisles so that the specially designed food carts could not be used in the economy sections without blocking all traffic. After unproductive efforts to channel passenger traffic into one aisle while serving trays used the other, this "bug" was eliminated by discarding the food carts and adding stewardesses to resume the old practice of serving on individual trays directly from the galley.

After the blunder of the miscarried container with sixty pieces of passenger luggage, baggage is now being delivered with less waiting on the part of passenger claimants and, of at least equal importance, with thirty percent fewer complaints of damage.

While airport and terminal facilities always lag behind civil air transportation's requirements, improvisation eased many situations in 1970; and more effective and efficient permanent facilities were to come into use in 1971 and later.

Airplane and particularly engine "bugs" resulted in spotty and unsatisfactory "on-time" performance in the 747's first year. With the successive months, operations became smoother and smoother in the "breaking-in" process. With a conservative policy of taking no chances whatsoever with safety, delays though disagreeable and often painful were inevitable. As the airplane and the engines began to settle into their groove of dependability, the on-time record of Pan Am's 747 operation improved.

Security requirements which were never envisioned when the 747 was conceived in 1965 or when terminals were laid out have caused delayed departures and added unreliability. While passengers have generally understood and endorsed baggage search and other security measures as protection against hi-jacking, no one enjoys such delays but no one has devised methods of eliminating them completely without far greater delay and hazard of a forced deviation into Cuba or, as it happened, Cairo.

One technological advance created much trouble. To save weight by utilizing new techniques, the electrical circuits to each passenger seat involved in individual selection among several varieties of stereo music, to turn on or off the movie audio, to call the stewardess, and to adjust the reading light were channeled into a single cable by a "multiplex" system. In spite of contractors' guarantees and warranties, this sophisticated process initially produced results that ranged from perfection to hilarity or extreme exasperation. More than once on early flights, sudden on-screen movie noises turned on or off all cabin lights, tinkled the call bells, and winked on or off the stewardesses' call lights, all in cadence with the sharp sounds of the movie. Most passengers found that an hour or so of such aberration was not at all amusing. Pan Am and the subcontractors' electrical engineers did very little sleeping while "multiplex" was becoming an increasingly dirty word.

Both Boeing and Pan Am have been pleased and even surprised that no "bugs" developed in the flying qualities or the flight control systems of their big new airplane. As is the practice with new automobiles, power has been provided for all controls handled by the pilot. Some were powerful hydraulic controls and others were large pneumatic controls each governed by electrical servo-motors. These systems were established in duplicate so that one system would remain operative if another failed. The imaginative new inertial guidance system which replaced the human navigator in the 747 was itself a complex of computers, gyroscopes, and intricate equipment. The fact that controls and guidance have all worked smoothly and no "bugs" were uncovered to appreciably affect the cockpit was gratifying to all and a tribute to the inventiveness, design, and production of Boeing and the engineers of the many subcontractors.

On the first anniversary of the commercial operation of the 747, Pan Am published the steady improvement of the on-time record of its 747s. Pan Am recognized that the worst of the delays occurred at the peak of the summer travel season when the maximum number of Pan Am passengers were trying the 747 for the first time. The airline recognized that its task was to win back those passengers who suffered through some of the 747's growing pains.

In his public statement at the end of the 747's first year of service, the President of Pan Am Mr. Najeeb E. Halaby concluded:

> Most of the penalties and problems are behind us. We now have far more experience with the 747 than any other carrier, and the experience should work to our advantage in the future.
>
> We predict that the 747 will prove to be the most efficient flying machine in history. It will be the wings of a whole new system of total transportation from door to door or dock to dock. It will also serve as a new base for resuming the growth of airline earnings.

Whether or not the staggering businessman's risk taken by Mr. Allen of Boeing and Mr. Trippe of Pan Am in 1965 for the decade of the '70s will prove to be a success, failure, or draw could not be determined after only the first year of operation. The fact that most of the leading scheduled air carriers of the world and some of the supplemental and charter operators also bought 747s was an optimistic clue as to worldwide business opinion.

A few conclusions were evident after the first year of operations.

Neither Boeing nor Pan Am were bankrupt.

Where there were four thousand five hundred transports in the world's airline fleets of 1958, five times as many passengers were carried in three thousand five hundred jet transports in 1970.

Status After Two Years in Service

Finding and Fixing the Bugs. Even the most skillful designers, the most expert engineers, and the most efficient operators know that a new airplane, a new engine, and new ancillary equipment will inevitably contain bugs that can be discovered only by extensive and prolonged flying under the whole gamut of worldwide operating conditions.

By the end of 1971 after almost two years of service in commercial operations, the 747 had been worked long enough and hard enough for Pan Am and Boeing to be reasonably sure that all the major bugs had been exposed. During those two years, those bugs had been not only discovered and analyzed but also fixed.

Boeing had delivered one hundred and sixty-six 747 aircraft to twenty-seven airlines by the end of 1971. Most of those aircraft were delivered to carriers in the United States. The twenty-seven included airlines in Asia, the Middle East, Africa, and Europe. The smallest delivery was one aircraft to Condor in West Germany. The largest by far was the delivery of twenty-eight 747s to Pan Am with more in the production line for Pan Am in 1972.

During those first two years, the total 747 fleet had accumulated 570,000 flying hours. As a significant comparison, only 250,000 flying hours had been accumulated by the total

707 fleet during its first two years. Having received the earlier deliveries, Pan Am had many of the high-time 747s. Thirty-eight aircraft had flown over 5000 hours and eight had exceeded 6000 hours. Engine hours totalled about 2,280,000 flying hours.

This great amount of regularly scheduled usage in heat and in cold, in smooth fair weather and turbulent foul weather, in long and short and heavy and light flights from long and smooth and short and rough runways in the course of the two years gave to Boeing, Pratt & Whitney, Pan Am, and the other operators reason to believe that the inevitable bugs had been brought to light. And, of course, as quickly as bugs were identified, corrections or fixes were initiated.

One indication of the operational capability of a fleet of airplanes is the average daily utilization which an airline can obtain from all the airplanes in its fleet. In January 1971 Pan Am averaged five hours of flying per day from each of its three and four-tenths 747 airplanes in contrast with the 9.97 hours from each of its fleet of well broken-in long-range 707 passenger airplanes. One year later Pan Am's fleet of twenty-four 747s were flying 8.28 hours per day versus 8.45 hours by its 707s. By January 1972 the 747s flew 9.93 hours, substantially more than the 7.62 hours produced by the established and big money making 707s. In preparation for heavy traffic in the summer of 1972, the fleet of thirty 747s flew 10.67 hours daily in May. Naturally airlines' schedules, lengths of their routes, and other factors can control utilization. The figures are cited to support the contention that the 747 was probably well debugged during its second year of operation by Pan Am. Any fleet of thirty 747s that can spend thirty times 10.67 hours per day in the air is not wasting its time and money earning capacity while being debugged in hangars and engineering or maintenance shops.

The Engines. Five major changes had been made in Pratt & Whitney's JT9D-3 engine, which became the JT9D-3A when those changes were retrofitted into the engine. Those and additional improvements were combined to produce the JT9D-7, which had increased thrust and substantially improved maintainability. The JT9D-7 was a programmed version in the growth process of the JT9 engine series.

By the end of 1971, the JT9D-7 had flown just over 13,000 hours with only two in-flight shutdowns and only one non-scheduled engine removal required. During its first 13,640 flying hours, the JT9D-3 experienced six inflight shutdowns and fourteen non-scheduled engine changes. In shutdown per 1000 engine hours, the JT9D-7's record was three times better than the JT9D-3's. In engine changes, the JT9D-7's rate was eight per 100,000 hours in contrast with the rate of 103 for the JT9D-3's.

Entertainment. In early operations, many passengers were aggravated by the erratic scrambling of several varieties of music and the movie-audio or by the total failure of their headsets to provide any sound at all. These annoyances were due to flaws in the cable system which had been designed to provide eight channels of sound as well as movie sound-track audio to each seat through a lightweight multiplex system designed to replace many miles of wiring in each airplane. While multiplex techniques were not new to the electronics industry, the 747 was the first commercial aircraft to utilize these techniques to any extent. These failures soured some early passengers on the 747.

Both Pan Am and Boeing insisted on vigorous emergency action by the manufacturer of the multiplex system. These errors were not easily corrected as the system was a highly complex one. To illustrate the complexity, each aircraft system consisted of 668 components, many of which were similar to small computers with hundreds of transistors in each. While such complexity was not desired, even less acceptable would have been the bulk and weight on every flight of many miles of direct (simplex) wiring. More precise equipment, more careful testing, and better installation finally resulted. The reliability of the multiplex system improved by eight hundred percent by the end of 1971.

Airframe Changes and Growth. The 747 airframe underwent eight minor changes. Some of these changes reduced the drag to the extent of 2.8 percent. Any reduction of drag happily produces improved performance and better economics. Several annoying delays had been caused by the inadvertent release of the big passenger emergency evacuation chutes. When that occurred, either a replacement chute had to be installed or the deployed chute had to be repacked and restored in its position in the airplane. Both took time and caused delays.

The FAA's insistence that the 747's maximum passenger load could be evacuated under emergency conditions (total black-out and half of the doors assumed to be unusable) in the same ninety seconds required of much smaller jet transports had necessitated the design of new, wide, and complicated passenger doors which not only served as entrances and exits but also contained automatic semi-explosive devices to eject and inflate huge evacuation chutes in the first very few of those precious ninety seconds. The redesign of elements of the system and better training of operations and maintenance personnel solved this annoying problem. Engine thrust reversers were changed to improve the reliability of the braking system, and the trailing edge flap complex was improved. A changed air inlet in the engine mount resulted in a noise reduction which Boeing measured as between twenty-five and forty percent even when the more powerful JT9D-7 engines were used.

In keeping with the growth program, and as new installations were proved out and crew training and experience progressed, the FAA during the second year certified the 747 for instrument landings with only 700 feet visibility. This step forward improved the airplane's schedule reliability. Further certification for fully automatic blind landing at suitably equipped airdromes was scheduled for the near future. With reduced drag and increased power, the FAA also authorized an increase in allowable take-off weight and the carriage of five hundred passengers, sixteen of whom could be seated on the upper deck. Boeing finished its fatigue tests on the test airframe at the factory. All components survived the scheduled 60,000 hours of scientifically simulated flight, and the testing was then resumed to assure that elements would "fail-safe" when they eventually and finally must fail.

As to overall 747 performance, in the first two years, 747s served seventy-five cities and carried 19,000,000 passengers. There were no disastrous crashes. The 747 fleet was never grounded. Pilots of many nations expressed more and more enthusiasm about the flying qualities of the airplane. 747 schedule reliability for the first six months of operation was eighty-one percent. (In other words, only nineteen percent of scheduled flights were delayed fifteen minutes or longer for mechanical reasons.) After one year, schedule reliability rose to eighty-nine percent; after a year and a half, it was ninety-two percent; and, for the last four months of '71, reliability was never lower than ninety-four percent.

Passenger Acceptability. While the technical, mechanical, and engineering reports after two vigorous years of operation indicate that the 747 gamble for the '70s would justify very good odds from the beginning of the decade, the records of passenger acceptability and economic performance were not all rosy.

At the beginning of 747 operations, passenger surveys showed enthusiasm for the airplane. In the spring of 1970, eighty-five percent of the 747 passengers said they preferred it to any other airplane. Then came failures in multiplex entertainment equipment, delayed departures due to incomplete or unorganized terminal facilities, delays due to accidentally deployed escape chutes, delays due to engine changes, quantities of lost baggage in large containers, and delays and inconveniences due to inadequately trained or experienced personnel. In the summer of 1970, passenger preference for the 747 dropped from eighty-five to seventy-six percent and in the winter of 1970-71 to seventy-one percent. Early in the second year, personnel training and experience moved up the learning curve, some bugs were fixed, reliability and service began to improve, and some unhappy passengers began to return to the 747. In the spring of '71, passenger preference for the 747 edged up to seventy-three percent and by the end of the 1971 summer it reached eighty-nine percent.

Business passengers did not like the 747 as much as the pleasure passengers. Of 3290 pleasure passenger respondents in early '71, 86.5 percent preferred the 747 over other jets, 51.4% strongly, 29% moderately, and 6.1% weakly. 2361 business passenger respondents reported that 81.2% preferred the 747, 38.5% strongly, 31.9% moderately, and 10.8% weakly. On North Atlantic routes in the summer of '71 when the loads were the heaviest, 64% of all categories of 747 passengers said they felt less fatigue in the big airplane, 32% felt about the same degree of fatigue in the 747 as in other jets, but only 4% felt more fatigue in the 747.

Within Pan Am, the decline in passenger acceptability after the first flush of enthusiastic and expertly advertized initiation was probably related not so much to in-flight service and the crews in the cockpit and cabin as it was to the problems of the Airport Services organization. During the first two years, almost 12,000 Pan Am employees at thirty-five bases had seen the 747 for the first time, attempted to provide temporary arrival facilities, and occasionally in rain or snow or great heat or deep cold handle extraordinarily large numbers of tired passengers, get huge baggage containers off and back on their seventeen-foot-high airplane decks, service a huge new airplane, clean it with its twelve toilets, reload it, and tow it out for takeoff in about thirty minutes. Not one of those thirty-five Pan Am bases, including—particularly—Pan Am's home base at JFK, had completed the massive construction needed to handle the 747 nor had adequately trained the bulk of airport personnel. Historically, airport construction and facilities have lagged behind the introduction of new aircraft. Normally, airport managers are municipal, state, or government authorities or administrators who cannot or do not get budget provisions for new facilities until the requirement is visible. On the part of the airlines, Boards of Directors may consider twenty-five million dollar airplanes but terminals or maintenance facilities costing as much as two airplanes generate long debates, restudies, and delays.

In the mid '60s, Mr. G. Erskine Rice had been transferred to Operations from Pan Am's Technical Services Staff, where he had proved to be a broadly capable number two man in Pan Am's program of training airlines in foreign countries, which were usually emerging undeveloped countries, in line with the concept of the Marshall Plan. He was elected a Vice-President and charged with establishing standards and obtaining uniformly high quality airport services in Pan Am's large number of airports which had grown up under several autonomous regional managers with no centralized operational authority of any kind. Vice-President Rice began molding into shape all the agencies at the airports which were under the control of his chief, the Senior Vice-President, Operations. However, most of the services which had contact with passengers at the airports reported directly or through separate channels either to the Senior Vice-President-Marketing, the Senior Vice-President-International Affairs, or the Vice-President–Public Relations. It was about the time when preparations to handle the 747s became urgent that the elementary requirement that there be one Pan Am chief of all Pan Am activities at each Pan Am airport became evident even to the old timers in Pan Am who had originally run each region as their own separate airline in the days of DC-3s and Flying Boats. Vice-President Rice finally became the Pan Am chief of all Airport Services with over 12,000 employees at 129 airports, and Pan Am's services to 747 passengers at thirty-five of those airports began uniformly to improve.

In 1971, the claims Pan Am received for lost or damaged baggage were fourteen and one-half percent fewer than in 1970 and twenty-eight percent fewer than in 1969. In October, 1971 Pan Am paid just over $100,000 in baggage claims. In October a year earlier, the figure was $160,000. In 1971 overall passenger complaints (personnel attitude, baggage handling, delays, facilities, seat assignments, etc.) were 10.4 percent fewer than in 1970 while passenger commendations increased 30.6 percent in 1971. A very important improvement was a 55 percent improvement in On Time Departures (delays, if any, less than fifteen minutes) by Pan Am's 747s from January to December 1971. An important part of this big step forward can be credited to a sharp improvement in Airport Services of all types.

Economic Results. Economic considerations will of course determine whether or not the 747 gamble was a winner or a loser. Without doubt, like all its predecessors, the 747 will make more money after its break-in period. If it could break even in 1971 or 1972, it should be a moneymaker in the mid-70s and perhaps a bonanza in the late '70s.

Passenger traffic across the North Atlantic in 1970 and 1971 was much lighter than forecast for a number of reasons including the unanticipated economic recession of that period. The 747s on those most heavily travelled and usually most remunerative routes were far from filled. CAB data indicates that the most heavily travelled airline averaged two hundred and forty-six passengers per 747; the least heavily travelled, one hundred and seventy-four passengers; and the median, two hundred and four. Again however, the CAB data shows that the 747 did well in comparison with the 707. TWA's and Pan Am's combined reports stated that they carried more than twice as many revenue passengers in their 747s as they carried in their long range fan-jet 707s. This proportion was due in part to scheduling.

Air cargo was proportionately even less plentiful than air passengers in '70 and '71. The huge cargo holds below the passenger decks in the 747s were very far from filled. CAB data for the months of July and August 1971 recorded only 3300 pounds of cargo on the average U.S. domestic flight of the 747s, 8100 pounds on the North Atlantic routes, and, due largely to the outbound loads to our military units in the Pacific, 12,300 pounds average, all routes, both ways in the Pacific Area. Even those Pacific loads were less than one quarter of the 747's capacity.

By the end of 1971, Boeing's stock and the stock of its airline customers had not recovered from the market break of 1970. Pan Am reported a loss of 48,000,000 dollars in 1970 and 45,500,000 dollars in 1971. Quite clearly, no one was getting rich on the 747. On the other hand, Boeing analyzed the available CAB data reported by U.S. operators of 747s and has published conclusions that those operators were much better off for having operated Boeing 747s than they would have been had their operations been limited to Boeing 707s.

In its first two years, the 747 did not produce the sharp reduction in operating costs from the level of the best 707 (the long range fan-jet 707-320B) that the designers and developers hoped to attain. From the raw data reported by the five major U.S. airlines that operated both types, it was computed that the direct operating cost of the 747 was $3.73 per mile while the 707 cost $1.83 per mile. These figures resolve into a cost of 0.977 cents per seat per mile of flight for the 747 and 1.189 cents per seat-mile for the 707. These data indicate that the 747 operated only eighteen percent more economically than the 707 per seat-mile.

A substantial proportion of the failure of the 747 to operate more economically was the high cost of engine maintenance during the period of debugging the JT9D-3 and developing the JT9D-7. Where the JT9D-3 cost as much as $142.00 for maintenance per flight hour, it was anticipated that, by the end of 1971, JT9D-7's maintenance cost would drop to $90.00 per flight hour. This figure will compare to a cost of $40.00 per flight hour for the 707's engine, the JT3D, at the same stage of growth. The JT9D-7 will produce more than two and a half times as much thrust as the JT3D.

Airframe maintenance costs during these first two years were higher than planned for average years in the life of the airplane. CAB reports show that 747 airframe maintenance cost $120.00 per flight hour compared to $82.00 for the 707 at the same stage.

Boeing concluded that the direct maintenance costs of the 747 totalled 0.10 cents per seat-mile while the 707 now costs 0.14 cents per seat-mile, which gives the 747 a twenty-eight percent advantage.

The indirect costs (galley service, airplane cleaning, toilet service, handling cargo and baggage at the airplane, and like items) are more difficult to compute and more subject to controversy than the direct costs. Boeing computes the cost of the indirects for the 707 at 0.321 cents per seat-mile and for the 747 at 0.225 cents per seat-mile. The 747 would then be 29.9 percent more economical than the 707 on that criterion.

Even with these reductions in costs, the airlines lost money in '70 and '71. Boeing maintains that the losses would have been greater if the operators had not had 747s. Boeing said: "747s have flown ninety-six billion seat-miles since start of service. If the same number of seat-miles had been flown by 707s, industry operating costs would have increased by approximately $200,000,000."

Futures? One clue to the future of the 747 sheds a most rosy glow over the promise of that great gamble for the 1970s. In spite of the competition of Douglas' and Lockheed's big wide-bodied tri-jets and probable competition by the British-French Concorde and the Russian TU 44 supersonic transports, the Boeing Company is operating on a program to sell between eight hundred and one thousand 747 passenger, freighter, and convertible models before 1980. To buy those aircraft, Pan Am and other airlines will need a return to the rates of growth in the decade of the sixties, for traffic by both passengers and cargo, and some increase in tariffs to meet wage and salary increases as well as to offset overall inflation and the great burden of the high interest they have had to pay by borrowing funds in 1969 and 1970 to purchase their initial 747s. Boeing appears to be confident that all or most of these improved conditions will be forthcoming.

As time goes on, the stakes in the 747 gamble get higher and higher. By the middle of the decade, Pan Am, or Boeing, or both may cash in on a great win or take an enormous loss.

The 747 venture is still the great air transport gamble of the seventies.